Copyright © 2015 by Melissa Griffin and Dr. Loretta Rhoads

All Rights Reserved

ISBN-13: 978-1515115489

ISBN-10: 1515115488

Pilgrim, You'll Go Far

Pilgrim, You'll Go Far

INTRODUCTION

I would like to dedicate this project, first and foremost, to my Savior, Jesus Christ. Without His guiding hand, I would not still be alive to share my experiences. He is the most important Counselor I have. I treasure the Word that He is, the Word that is written and the Word that He speaks into my heart and life. He is my strength.

I want to thank Dr. Loretta Rhoads, a.k.a. "Mama Loretta," for her countless hours of input into my life. She has not only counseled me on the contents of this book and been a part of their writing, but she has also been an inspirational mentor to my life. God knew what He was doing when He put my life together with Dr. Rhoads. If it were not for her consistency of pushing me out of my comfort zone, I would not be who I am today. Thank you, Mama Loretta!

To my husband, I want to say thank you for always being proud of me and encouraging me to do all that I am able to do. You are, without question, my rock, and I love you with all my heart. I waited a long time for you, and I'm so glad I did! God gave me the best when He gave me you.

To my parents and grandparents, thank you for the consistent lives you have lived. Thank you for pouring into me the truths of God's Word. Thank you for not only teaching them to me, but also living them in front of me. The fact that you are more than just words is a treasure to my life. You have invested time, prayer, sleepless nights and fasting into my life. I am happy to say that they have not returned void to you. You have my utmost respect and love. I know that you are proud of me and believe in me and for that, I smile.

To my countless number of friends and supporters I would like to say thank you. To those of you that have driven hours to hear me preach, I would like you to know that I am humbled by that. To those of you that support our ministry, both financially and prayerfully, I cannot say enough to thank you for being a part of what God has called us to do.

"PILGRIM, YOU'LL GO FAR!"

When I was a teenager one of the prophets in my home church gave me an encouraging word. "Pilgrim," he called me, "You'll go far." This became a common phrase that he would say throughout my teenage years. I always loved it when he would speak it to me, but I never quite knew what he meant. For one thing, the term, "Pilgrim," is not a commonly used one. So, the phrase stuck in my heart and mind.

One occasion I will never forget was during our annual youth camp the year I was seventeen. There was an incredible outpouring of the Holy Ghost in the church service and I was lost in the Spirit for hours as the Presence of God filled the auditorium that night. I remember coming back to the awareness of my surroundings after the service had already been dismissed. There were only a few of us left in the church building. I remember, as I lay there across the church pew, hearing Bro. Bradford walk up beside the pew and say, "Pilgrim, you'll go far!" This time when he said it, I began to weep. I knew he was speaking by the Spirit of God about my future. Although I still didn't completely understand what it meant, I knew God was letting me know that He had a plan for me, a plan that would take me far, farther than I could imagine.

MY PARENTS

I am an extremely blessed individual. God could not have given me better parents than Paul and Cathy Turman. I can honestly say that I have no memories of hearing my parents fuss with each other when I was a child. They are best friends until this very day. It has always been a comfort and strength to have parents like them.

My Dad has always been my hero. I wrote a paper in second grade English class on how I was going to be just like my dad, even to the extent of being a firefighter like him. Dad always made time for us and loved to play with us. My Dad is a man's man, but my Dad is also a sensitive man. I remember the day before I was to leave for my first trip to India. I had so many different feelings and emotions I didn't know whether to be scared or explode with excitement. My Dad came to my little apartment bringing something for me to take on the trip. After taking what he had brought to me, I flung my arms around his neck and we both stood there in the doorway crying. My Dad spoke the same words then that he has said so many times during new seasons of my life. He said, "Your mom and I dedicated you to the Lord as a baby, and we do it all over again right now."

My mom is the kind of person that anyone would want to talk to. Mom and I have always been friends. I remember as a teenager going shopping with her. We would hear other mothers with their teenage daughters fighting in the store over something. I could never understand how a daughter could speak to her mother in such a way. I would always tell mom that I was glad we were friends. It was probably more of a challenge for my mom to believe that I would go to the nations than it was for anyone. She knew how that from the time I was a baby I didn't want to be separated from the safety of my parents. She knew that I never wanted to stay away from home, even for one night, with friends. As a young girl I would sometimes tell her, "My friend asked me to stay the night, but I don't want to, so will you please just say no?" Mom knew that it was definitely going to have to be a God thing for her baby girl to go far away from home.

If there was ever a girl who loved her mom and dad, it is me. I honor them and the place they have always walked in, not only individually, but also together as man and wife. I have always said I wanted to have a marriage like they have. Although the path the Lord has led me down over the past ten years has often taken me far from home, my parents have never relented on their desire to see me fulfill all that God has purposed for me to do. They have offered Godly counsel when situations presented themselves that I did not know how to handle. They have prayed a countless number of prayers for me as I have traveled the world, and lost plenty of hours of sleep on my behalf. They have pushed back their plate and fasted for my safe return. They have remained faithful to God in their own lives and callings all the years that I have been alive. It is no doubt that I am a blessed individual having Paul and Cathy Turman as my Dad and Mom.

GROWING UP WITH GOD

I can think back through my growing up years and make stops along the way at moments when experiences with God changed my life. As a seven year old child I was "slain in the Spirit" in a camp meeting service. I do not know how long I was out in the Spirit, but I remember when I came to myself I was lying on the floor weeping with my little hands straight in the air and mouth stammering. My mother was kneeling beside me weeping and my older sister was standing there crying and praying over me as well.

A few years down the road, I saw Jesus. I was thirteen years old. For several nights I stayed the night with my sister, Rebekah, while her husband was away on a construction job. On this particular night, I was very excited because the next morning my Sunday School class from church was taking a big trip to Branson, Missouri, to see a live play about the life of Jesus called "The Promise." I went to sleep that night anxious for the morning trip not knowing that during the night I would have a dream that would impact me forever. In the dream I was sitting in my normal seat at church listening to a preacher. I turned to my right and Jesus was sitting in the seat beside me. My eyes became huge as I realized who I was seeing. He did not say a word. He just looked at me. He looked at me with those eyes that cannot be given a description. Then, he held out His precious hands to me. I saw the holes in His hands where the nails had pierced Him and put my fingers over them. I then looked back up in to the face of Jesus. He did not say a word. He just smiled and His smile said more than a million words. That was the end of my dream. In the morning, I was so moved with emotion that I was hardly able to talk to anyone. I remember sitting in a seat by myself and going over in my mind the experience from the night before as we headed to Branson on our big Silver Eagle church bus. We reached the Branson theatre and were taken to our seats. My seat happened to be on the aisle. I did not know that during the play, the actors would be coming down the aisle putting the audience right in the middle of the story. Toward the end of the show, the actor portraying Jesus came struggling down the aisle carrying the cross toward the stage where he would be crucified. My seat, being on the aisle, put me only inches from this man acting as Jesus. I was sobbing so hard that I could not catch my breath. The experience in the dream the night before was making the 'play' very real to me. As we were exiting the theatre, I remember seeing my red and swollen tear streaked face in a mirror. I did not stay around to shake hands with the actors like everyone else. I went back to the bus, crawled into my seat and cried some more. On the way home, I told my Sunday school teacher, Sister Janna, the reason why I was crying so hard and why I had not been able to stop crying since leaving Branson. She was wonderful and prayed with me, encouraging me to continue to let the Lord work in my life. I have never forgotten that experience of seeing Jesus. Everything in me longs for the day when I will see Him again.

As I grew, my longing for the things of God also grew. I would hear my mentors tell stories about seeing visions and angels and it would stir up a deep hunger in me to have those experiences as well. I wanted them. I asked for them. As I look back, I remember a rather humorous moment in my search for God. I was fourteen years old. I would typically spend time in prayer after lying down in my bed, but on this night, I knelt beside the bed with my back to the open room. I began to talk to God about letting me see His angels. I was asking why other people got to see them but I did not. I was asking Him to please open my eyes to see in the spirit. All of the sudden, the Presence of God filled my room. I knew there was a huge angel standing behind me and all I had to do was turn around to see. Instead of turning around, however, I crawled into the bed as fast as I could and covered my head with the blanket. After a few minutes I did not sense that consuming Presence of God anymore. I barely peeked out over the top of the blanket, and when I saw nothing, threw them back aggravated with myself that I had been afraid. I started telling God that if He would just send His angel back I wouldn't hide again. If I had a guess, I would say that Heaven might have been laughing at that moment.

Another moment with God in my room was in the middle of the night. I was still a young teenager at the time, though I cannot say exactly how old I was. I was in a deep sleep in my bed when one of those 'suddenly' experiences happened. I was jolted awake out of my sleep. My eyes popped open. I was as wide awake as If I had never been asleep. As soon as my eyes opened I heard these words, "God is in your room." There was an intense heat in my room and a weight of God's Presence so strong that it felt like I was being pushed down into my bed. I do not know how long this experience with God lasted, but I have never forgotten it. As soon as the Presence of God lifted, I almost instantly went back into a deep sleep.

THE MISSING CHUNK

I remember weeping before God at the altar in my Papaw's church at the age of five. I remember this being the moment I gave my heart to Jesus. I should tell you now that my Papaw is one of God's giants, at least, that is the way I have always seen him. As pastor of our church, he would always try to bring in men and women of God who were full of faith and power. Since I am the youngest of the six grandkids in our family he calls me the "Last of the Mohicans." I always made sure that I was in his arms at the end of church services so he could introduce me as "The Mohican" to all the visiting ministers. After the introduction I considered them my personal friends as well. I remember a missionary who worked in South Africa that came to our church time and time again. I was a very young girl but I remember loving that missionary greatly.

Pilgrim, You'll Go Far

I was one of those children who never wanted to be away from home. If there ever were two special people in my life it would be my mom and dad, Paul and Cathy Turman. They are the associate pastors of our church alongside my dad's father. One of the elders in our church, Bro. Ronnie Faulkner, who has already gone Home to be with the Lord, related to my parents a story about us kids one time. My older sister, brother and I always wanted to stay with Bro. Ronnie and his wife if my parents went somewhere without us because Bro. Ronnie owned a Sonic and that was a very big deal to us! We would get to eat at Sonic every day. So, on one such occasion when my parents went to a conference, we stayed at the Faulkner's house. They came in to check on us in the bedroom that night, and all three of us were huddled in a big bed, hugging each other and crying for our mommy and daddy!

Having grown up in one of the greatest churches ever founded, I had many experiences with God by the Holy Ghost. I remember, as a seven year old girl, being slain in the Spirit for an hour or more. I can recall prayer meetings with my friends when we would be so lost in prayer that we would never make it into the main church service. One year, during our annual youth camp, I was filled with the power of the Holy Ghost. The youth minister, Bro. Jerry Faulkner, Jr., told me later that every few minutes it sounded like the language I was praying in would totally change to another language. I believe God was preparing me then to go into the nations of the world.

I prayed all throughout my childhood years to know what the will of God was for my life. My plan was to get married as soon as I graduated from high school and have a family. This was not really possible because at the time I graduated I did not have a boyfriend nor did I have any prospects of one. I became depressed. I was earnestly praying to know the will of God, but it seemed like a chunk was missing from the picture of what I was to do with my life. After graduation I spent two years working in our church school as a teacher's aid and I helped my Mamaw in the church kitchen. My Mamaw is a faithful and true woman of God. One word that comes to mind when thinking of my Mamaw is 'faithful.' I am named after my Mamaw and have always been her baby girl as well. It was a privilege to work with Mamaw and we would cook lunch every day for the men that worked on the property. I would wash what seemed to be an endless number of dishes. I remember one such day when I was bent over the big industrial sink washing dishes that I had this thought, "Lord, am I going to wash dishes for the rest of my life?!" I know, looking back things weren't the way I perceived them to be, but to an eighteen year old girl searching for God's purpose in her life, it seemed like a trial.

I continued working with my Mamaw, helping in the school, going through our Bible College courses, praying, and waiting on God. When I was nineteen years old my Papaw met and invited a missionary lady to our church. She was a single lady in her 60's doing a great work in the nation of India. My heart was drawn to her and I loved her instantly. The next day we had lunch together in the church fellowship hall. My mom, the missionary lady and I all sat around the table talking about India when suddenly she looked at me and said, "I think I would like to take you to India with me sometime." I was a little shocked by that but my response was, "I think I would go." I remember looking over at my mom's face when I said that. Her eyebrows were raised and she had the expression on her face that read, "Yeah, right." She knew how much of a 'home-body' I had always been and did not see any way that I would actually go to India.

That conversation took place in April of 2004. I did not see that missionary again until August of the same year but what she said to me never left my mind or my heart. It plagued me until it was the last thought in my mind every night. I would awaken suddenly in the middle of the night praying for her in India. I would also wake up with my heart racing in the morning and India would be the very first thought in my mind. I lived those months with perpetual butterflies in my stomach just thinking of what it might be like to actually be a missionary. This lady came back to our church in August for our annual Camp meeting. After she finished speaking one night my Papaw gave an altar call. He started with my age group. I heard him saying, "If you are in the Single's class and you will dedicate your life as a missionary, whether it be at home or abroad, I want you to come up here. But," he said, "don't come yet." He then proceeded to give the same challenge to the teenage group, and then to the juniors. I couldn't wait for him to get finished and to say, "Now, if that is you, come up here!" My heart was literally in my throat and pounding so hard I didn't know if I would be able to stay in my seat until he was finished. Finally he said to come and I went forward as fast as I could. That particular night is one of the great moments that I can look back to in my life.

    A few weeks later after some sleepless nights I talked to my Papaw, who is my Pastor, about going to India. I will never forget what he said, "Sis, it is always a good idea for anyone to go to the mission field. Now, whether that is what you do with your entire life is between you and God, but it is always a good idea to go at least once." I was thrilled to hear this! From that day forward I began to plan on actually going to the mission field. I talked with the missionary and told her that I would like to go and that I would stay the entire amount of time that she did. It was miraculous how the money was there for my passport, visa, plane ticket and then money to live on while I was gone. God provided over three times as much money as I needed without me asking anyone for it.

And so, on March 14, 2005, I left the Little Rock, Arkansas, airport with two missionary ladies in their 60's. I would not be back home for two and a half months, did not really know the people I was going with, had never been in an airplane, and was a pretty scared and excited 20 year old girl, but I knew that I had found the missing chunk in my life.

WILL YOU DIE FOR ME?

During the months prior to going to India I did much praying. I was living alone at that time because my roommate had recently married. At that time, all of the friends I grew up with were newly married and starting families, so I had a lot of time to spend on my own. The Lord's Presence was so sweet during those days of preparation for India. It was at night when I would lay down to sleep that He would begin to talk to me. I spent many of those nights weeping in His wonderful Presence. One night I began to feel unworthy of the task ahead of me. I didn't know how I was going to minister to India seeing as I was so young and without any kind of experience in that arena. I kept saying, "Lord, I am unworthy to go to India." The Lord's reply to me was precious. He said, "Melissa, I don't use you because of your worthiness. I use you because of your willingness." I cried out to Him that if anything I was definitely willing for Him to use me!

Another such night while weeping in the Presence of the Lord, I heard Him speak. What He said was not an easy thing for a young person to hear. He softly asked me the question, "Will you die for Me?" When I heard this, my heart was broken. My eyes overflowed like fountains. I could not speak. I knew that in just a few short weeks I would be leaving my home and everyone that I loved so dearly. I did not have any idea what to expect in India. The idea of being killed for the sake of the Gospel was very real to me. I wept bitterly thinking of all my personal dreams for the future. The Lord asked me several more times the same question, "Will you die for Me?" It was not an easy decision because the reality of India was staring me in the face. I knew it was very possible that I could die for the Lord in just a few weeks. After much sorrow I said yes to the Lord. Looking back, I see how I did die for Him. I died to my will. I died to everything I had ever planned for my life. I died to Melissa and said yes to God's plan for Melissa. To this day it continues to be an adventure with God.

THE DAY I MET 'MAMA LORETTA'

March, 14, 2005

The day had finally arrived. I was headed to India for the first time. I was traveling with a special lady named, Mary Ann Johnston. Mary Ann had mentioned to me the day before leaving that there would be another lady going to India with us. As I reached the airport that day with my parents, grandparents and best friend, I was very scared. First of all, I had never been on an airplane. Secondly, I was leaving everything I knew. I clutched my little travel pillow tightly as I said goodbye to my loved ones and walked away with Mary Ann. As we reached our departure gate, I saw a woman sitting there reading her Bible. As we approached, she looked up and smiled. After being introduced this lady looked at Mary Ann and said, "Mary Ann, are you out of your mind? What in the world are you thinking bringing a beautiful girl like this to India? We are both going to have to carry big sticks to protect her." This lady, whom I did not yet know, had just eased some of the tension that I was feeling by making me laugh. Little did I know that this lady would become 'Mama Loretta.'

Her name is Loretta Rhoads. Actually, it is Doctor Loretta Rhoads. She is an accomplished, educated and beautiful lady. She had been on many mission's trips before as she is forty years my elder. She always liked to stay in a room alone if possible on trips because she is awake all through the night praying and reading the Word of God. In all of my life I have never seen anyone who loves the Word of God like she does. After first meeting her, I was amazed as I watched her read the Bible. She would open the Word and within moments tears would be dripping off of her face onto the pages. I remember thinking, "I wish I felt that way when I read the Bible. "

On this trip to India, it was not possible for Dr. Rhoads to have a room to herself. Mary Ann spoke to Dr. Rhoads and told her that she had to stay in a room with me. Dr. Rhoads tells that she was just, "doing what she had to do." The first night after arriving in India, Dr. Rhoads says that when she came out of the wash room she saw me lying across the bed weeping and praying. She says that at that moment she knew it was going to be okay to share a room with me.

I watch people. I watch their actions and reactions. I notice things that others sometimes miss. After watching Dr. Rhoads, I knew that I wanted to be like her. She was a pastor's wife, a pianist, a teacher, a prayer warrior, a marvelous singer, funny, witty, a missionary, etc… By the time we had been in India for two weeks I knew who this woman was. One morning, in the state of Nagaland, I was not feeling well and did not go to the Bible school classes. During break time, Dr. Rhoads hurriedly came into the room to get a notebook and turned around to leave. As she did I spoke up and said, "Sister Loretta?"

"Yes?" she said.

"You are everything I have ever wanted to be," I replied.

With a shocked look she said, "I didn't even know you were watching me."

From that day forward, Dr. Rhoads became 'Mama Loretta.'

It was a great comfort to my Mom to know that there was a 'Mama' in India watching out for her girl. Mama Loretta and I laughed so much during those subsequent weeks in India. One evening we were talking and decided that neither one of us had ever laughed as much, cried as much or prayed as much with any one person as we had with each other. There have been many days that have passed now since meeting Dr. Rhoads. To each other we are no longer Dr. Rhoads and Melissa.

To me she is 'Mama Loretta,' and to her I am 'Missy.'

From that day to this, God has knit our hearts together like David and Jonathan, or like Elijah and Elisha. The Bible says that we should go out "two by two." This is so if you encounter trouble, you will find strength in the person you are with. Even though she is 40 years my elder, Loretta Rhoads and I have traveled this world preaching the Gospel of Jesus Christ! God put her in my life on my first trip to India to show me once again that His plans are higher than mine! She has become my spiritual mother and mentor and I will be forever grateful to God for causing our two separate paths to connect and become one path.

TWO WORLDS

Year: 2005

My first trip to India opened a new world to me, not just in the natural but also in the Spirit. Within the first week of being in India, I began to see visions. I was familiar with visions because of the teaching in the Word of God and because of the way I was raised, but they were not something that had ever happened in my life.

The Lord opened my eyes on the day we went to see the Commissioner of Nagaland. We were there to request entrance papers into his state in far Eastern India. I was excited about the opportunity of visiting with a government official. We were greeted warmly as we entered his office. He finished a last minute phone call, and then had tea and refreshments brought in. The Commissioner was a great man of God and a Spirit-filled Believer. I realized that I had been trembling since entering his office. Suddenly, the Lord showed me a vision. I saw the Commissioner with a large machete' in his hand. He was cutting a path through a field and telling people to follow him. It was a short vision but it had a great impact on me. We had a powerful time of prayer together that day. I was still trembling from the power of God as we got into our taxi to leave. I sat silently in the backseat looking out the window and watching the scenes of every day India pass by. I finally began to share with Sister Loretta and Sister Maryann about the vision. They immediately saw great significance in it. They told me that the Commissioner was able to open up the path for many to go into Nagaland. They also told me that the Naga people actually do use big machetes to cut down tall grass. I did not personally know this, but God did and He was showing me just how precisely he was beginning to speak to me. From that day until now, I have learned to pay close attention to the visions of the Spirit.

SPEAK ENGLISH!

March 2005

We were on our way to Nagaland. We had already completed the airplane ride which took us halfway there. We then had to catch a train and ride it for six hours to go the rest of the way. There was nothing out of the ordinary happening. We had bought some green coconuts at the pit stop and drank the juice inside. I was enjoying watching the scenery go by when all of the sudden five men burst into our berth of the train. The only thing different was that these men were all dressed as women. In India, there is a large class of men that are eunuchs. They have formed colonies where they live together as a class of people. Indians are afraid of them and believe that if they don't give the eunuchs money that a curse will be placed on their life. It is also believed that it is good fortune to bring a eunuch dressed as a woman and have them dance at a ceremony to bless a new born child.

    I did not know all of these things about eunuchs until later. All I knew was that these five men, dressed as women, pulled open the curtain of our berth and began demanding money. Our interpreter told them to go away, but they were adamant and belligerent. One of the leaders began to clap his hands toward our interpreter and act like he was putting a curse on all of us. Suddenly, the seasoned missionary lady we were traveling with, who had been sound asleep in her seat, came up out of her sleep and her seat shaking her finger in their faces and speaking in tongues. The entire group of eunuchs became very afraid and didn't know what to do. After a few moments of Holy Ghost tongues the leader said to Sis. MaryAnn, "Speak English! Speak English!" They were so frightened by what happened that they turned around and ran away! We never saw then again.

To this day, I would love to know what the Holy Ghost said to them!

OH GOD, BLIND THE POLICEMEN'S EYES

MARCH 2005

It was dark, raining and I was about to illegally jump off the backside of a train. When I reached India on that first trip I thought I was exhausted, but as I stood on the train waiting to jump, adrenaline surged through me. I heard the young man who came to meet us pray, "Oh, God, please blind the eyes of the policemen." My heart was racing and so was my mind. I didn't know what to expect in the area we were traveling to and emotions I had never experienced were flooding through me. I must confess that my faith was being tested strongly. God had been asking me before going on this trip if I would be willing to die for Him, and as I stood there on the train I decided surely this must be what He had been talking about. I had only been in India for one week of the two and a half months that I planned to stay. At that moment, it appeared that my life was coming to an end, and that my work in missions was to be short-lived.

We were traveling to Dimapur, Nagaland, on the far eastern side of India. Nagaland has always been a controversial state in the nation. As foreigners, we needed a group of four to qualify for entrance permits, but there were only three of us. Commissioner Aiyer, our Christian brother in the government office, told us to proceed with buying our airplane and train tickets to Dimapur and he would work on getting special permits for our group of three. When the day came for us to travel, the Commissioner informed us that he still did not have our permits, yet he counseled us to proceed with our plans. He told us he would personally go to the main office, push to get the permits and then fax them ahead of us to the young man we were to meet named, Yimso. Yimso planned to be at the station when the train pulled in. He would be waiting at the door of our railcar, and when we stepped off the train would walk with us into the police office with our permits. This was the plan, but plans do not always work. At the halfway point of our journey to Nagaland, we received a phone call from the Commissioner. He informed us that, in spite of his best effort, he was not able to get our permits that day. He said that the plans had once again been changed. It was at this moment I began to feel concern creeping into my heart. If we were caught trying to enter Nagaland illegally, we would at the least be banned from ever going back. We could not let that happen because a great work was being done there. We were going to teach and help with a new Bible school and church. I found myself thinking, "Oh no! Are we facing yet another change in plans?" It seemed that the certainty I had felt about going on this trip was flying out the window.

The new plan involved Yimso meeting us at a different station. One hour before the Main Depot, the train would stop for sixty seconds at a little spot in the road. We were supposed to be standing by the door with our luggage ready to quickly get off the train. It would then take us three hours to drive rough, back roads to the location of the Bible School. We moved close to the door as we felt the train slowing down. Standing there with too much luggage we prepared for the quick exit. The train lurched to a stop, but instead of helping us get off the train, Yimso jumped on with us. The three of us were confused and began to question, "Yimso, what are you doing? We have to get off the train. We don't have entrance permits!" He was standing there dripping wet from the rain that was falling outside. "Let's get this luggage back to your seats," he said.

    We carted our luggage back down the narrow aisle of the railcar and listened as Yimso explained yet another change in plans. He told us how they had searched all day long to find someone who would loan a vehicle to come and pick us up. In spite of his efforts, no one had a vehicle for him and it just so happened that all taxis were on strike that day. Yimso looked at us and said, "Three of us came to this station on one motorbike, and I don't think six of us and all this luggage will fit for the trip back."

I had never been away from home, flown in an airplane, ventured into a foreign country, owned a passport, eaten strange food, or jumped off a train. In fact, I had never even ridden a passenger train. My short life was passing before my eyes. The questions in my mind were endless, but I sat there silent, scared, and wide-eyed as I listened to Yimso explain to us what we had to do next. There was no choice in the matter. We were headed to the Main Depot in Dimapur which was crawling with armed military guards. This was where the train stopped for the night. We had to get off this train! This would have been an opportune time for me to find my Bible and read Hebrews Chapter Eleven once again, even though I was almost certain those giants of faith had never jumped off a train.

      The two grandmothers and I received our instructions. When the train pulled into the Depot we were to jump off the dark side of the train in one minute or less. Yimso explained that there would be young men from the Bible School on the back side of the train waiting to assist us. It would be redundant for me to try and explain how my heart was stuck in my throat as the train slowed down for the last time. I was chosen to go first; (chosen by my traveling friends.) How special. Oh, and it was still raining outside. Somehow, in spite of my great fear, I did what I was told to do and made the ten foot drop to the ground without injury. Bible School boys grabbed my luggage and I simply followed these men I had never seen through the water and thick, black mud that was now coating my flip-flop clad feet. I turned to look behind me. One grandma named Loretta was crawling over concrete barriers, ripping her skirt as she went, and the other grandma named Maryann was dangling from the train. Let me explain: Maryann, who was trying to get off the train hit a slippery place with her foot and was hanging from a yellow bar on the side of the train while Yimso tried to catch her from below! Today this is all hilarious, but right then it was serious. In spite of everything, we all made it safely. After trekking in the rain and across an open muddy field, we stood under a small eave of a brick building. Yimso told us we had better get out from under the 60 watt light bulb because our white faces would shine too much. We edged ourselves around the corner of the building back into the rain and darkness, and then, it happened. My two missionary, grandmother friends totally lost their composure. I, who was still reeling from what I had just experienced, stood there silently waiting. However, to my left I heard snickering, and then full blown laughter. Loretta and Maryann collapsed into laughter. I suppose it was a release of all the emotions of the day. Suddenly, I turned to them and said, "Shhhhhhh, quiet!" There, not even ten feet from us, was a policeman carrying a very large rifle. He was so concerned, however, about getting inside out of the rain and the mud that he never saw nor heard three white women who were illegally standing a few feet away. At that moment I remembered Yimso praying on the train, "Oh God, blind the policemen's eyes."

A van finally came, picked us up and took us to the Bible School. I don't see any need in trying to explain how high my faith was at the end of that very long day. We reached the school and they brought us water and towels so we could clean up. One small bucket of hot water had never looked so good. After we all washed up and found something to eat, we sat laughing and crying together thinking of what God had done for us. The very next day we were handed a package. It was our entrance permits! We really do dwell under the shadow of the Almighty.

A NEW SONG!

YEAR: 2005

From the time I was a little girl I wanted to write songs. My dad wrote the most beautiful songs on earth as I was growing up and I wanted to be like him. I had been in India for approximately two weeks when God gave me my first song. I was actually feeling sick that morning and asked to be excused from going to the classes that day. As soon as I placed my head on the pillow and closed my eyes I heard a song. I sat up immediately and began writing down the words that I was hearing. I not only heard the words, but the melody as well. When Sister Loretta and Sister Maryann came back to the room they found me weeping in the Presence of the Lord. I began to sing the new song to them and they wept as well. The message of the song said that no matter how hard the journey gets there is someone who must hear the Gospel of Jesus Christ, and that with Christ it is always possible to reach them.

Five years after God gave me that song, I received a phone call from Far Eastern India. On the other end of the line I heard 30 orphan children, half the world away, whom I had never met, singing my song. I was speechless. Tears overwhelmed me. What a thrill it was to hear those tiny voices singing and all because God gave a new song!

CATCH OUR TAXI!

YEAR : 2005

It was early morning in India and we were headed to Ambala City, Haryana. All of our things were piled into a small taxi van and headed to the train station. With space in the van being limited, I placed my camera bag and music player underneath my seat. We had approximately a forty minute drive to the train station. You have to understand that the train stations in India are incredibly busy places. As we pulled up in front of the station, we realized that our train would be at the platform within a few minutes. We jumped out of our taxi, grabbed suitcases and quickly headed to catch our train. I had been standing in the station for a couple of minutes when I suddenly realized that in our haste to get out of the taxi I had forgotten my camera and music player under the seat. When I realized my mistake, Mudir, our interpreter, took off running to try to catch the taxi. As he took off, the three of us in the station joined hands and began praying that God would make it possible for my things to be retrieved. It seemed more than impossible for Mudir to find it, because all of the taxi vans at the station are identical in appearance and there are hundreds of them. Miraculously, Mudir remembered that he had called the taxi driver with his personal cell phone earlier in the day (which is something he did not usually do.) As he ran through the maze of taxis, he called the driver and found that he was just then exiting the station area out onto the highway.

It was about ten minutes later when Mudir came walking back up to us inside the station. His face was red and he breathing hard from running, but he had a beautiful smile on his face. He also had my camera bag and music player in his hand. Fortunately for us the arrival of our train was delayed nearly thirty minutes. It was truly a miracle!

FIVE FLASHES

YEAR: 2005

Conferences in India are always eventful because you have so many different people and spiritual worlds to deal with. There are almost always miracles that take place but you also see the manifestation of evil spirits. We had been holding a conference in the city of Ambala in the Northern part of India. On this particular morning, we were going to travel about an hour to another city called Patiala where we would begin another conference that same evening. We had breakfast at the home in which we were staying, but after eating I began to feel sick to my stomach. I went back to the room and lay down. The moment I closed my eyes I saw a vision. At the time I had no understanding of what it meant, but the meaning was to become very clear later in the day. In the vision I saw the skyline of a large city which I somehow knew to be in India. A very black cloud was slowly moving in and overtaking the daylight of the city. Then, inside the dark mass of cloud, I saw three bright orange flashes of lightning. Then I saw two more flashes of lightning, but they were not as bright as the first three. This was the end of my vision. I had no understanding so I got up and looked for Mama Loretta to talk to her about it. She had no immediate understanding either, but she has never discounted anything I have said to her about seeing in the Spirit. Mama Loretta's encouragement is what caused me to pay attention to things I was seeing in the Spirit in the first place. We prayed together concerning it and then began to pack our things to go to the city of Patiala.

We never stay in hotels in India. We always stay with the pastors or local families. Our experiences in India have been the rustic reality of how they live, eat, sleep and function day to day. However, in this particular city, we had to conduct the conference in the basement of a hotel because no other in the city was big enough to host it. Because of this, we chose to stay in the hotel to make it easier on everyone. As we walked into our room that afternoon, I had all but forgotten about my vision from earlier that morning. I had forgotten that is until we turned the television on in our room. We never have a television while in India. We thought that perhaps we could find an English news channel to see what we had missed hearing about going on in the world. What we found left me speechless. As soon as we turned the television on we began hearing reports of bombs that had been exploding in the city of New Delhi. The newscaster told of three bombs that had already exploded and then of two more bombs the police were able to find and disarm. I sat there on the bed saying, "That is what I saw this morning! There were three bright flashes of light over a large city taking over the daylight and two more flashes that were not very bright!" We immediately began to pray more and to try to reach one of our greatest evangelist friends in India, Brother Francis Jude. Brother Jude had been with us for the Ambala conference, but could not stay with us for the Patiala meeting. As we left that morning for Patiala, Bro. Jude headed in the opposite direction for New Delhi. We tried to reach him but to no avail. Finally, after many attempts, we reached our dear brother. We could hear the pandemonium on the other end of the line. Brother Jude told us that he was okay, but that it had been a close call. He was actually in the train station when one of the first three bombs exploded. He said it was chaos after that of people trying to escape and to determine what was happening. He was not injured. He only had an ear that was hurting him because of the loudness of the explosion.

    We then tried to reach more of our dear friends. A young couple by the name of Vivek and Rosie, who had lived in the same apartment with us at times, were living in the city of New

Delhi. We had the same trouble reaching them, but when we did, Rosie recounted a miraculous testimony of safety as well. Rosie told us that she had called for a motor rickshaw to come to her house and pick her up. She needed to go to the marketplace to buy food. Not many thing in India run on time, but motor rickshaws are not really notorious for running late because there are so many of them. If one doesn't come, you can easily and quickly find another one. However, Rosie was pregnant and did not need to go walking in the heat to find a ride. So she waited, and waited, and waited. Her ride never came. She began to wonder what was going on until the live reports started coming across the television. One of the bombs had exploded in the very market that Rosie was going to. Out of thousands of markets in New Delhi it was the very one where she would have been.

    As we began to hear these reports from our friends, I asked God why I had not understood how to pray to prevent the bombs from happening at all. The Lord said to me, "They are safe aren't they?" Yes, yes, our special friends and loved ones were safe. The vision had become clear. I learned from the experience of the five flashes to never discount something you have seen in the Spirit. Do not discredit it as being too much pizza you ate. Lives could be at stake.

Mr. Happy

YEAR: 2005

On one of our many trips returning to our base in New Delhi, India, something wonderful happened, although it did not start out as a wonderful experience. We were in the city of Ambala trying to come up with a reasonable solution to get six of us and a ton of luggage to our destination in New Delhi. One taxi came and tried to get our luggage on the rack atop the vehicle and into the back of the jeep, but it just would not fit. The taxi driver was getting aggravated and so were we. So, we unloaded the luggage and waited another hour until a different taxi came with a bigger luggage rack. The second driver, called "Mr. Happy", was somehow able to pack the luggage into the vehicle. There was very little room in the back of the jeep because of the luggage and Yimso, a Bible School director from Nagaland, India, kept insisting that I sit up front instead of on top of the luggage. I kept refusing and insisting that he sit up front between an evangelist and the driver. Later, I was so glad Yimso did. If it had been otherwise, a soul would have been lost. During our drive, Bro. Jude, the evangelist from South India, began to pray and worship the Lord and to sing in the Spirit. After a little while of this, Yimso began to speak in Hindi to our driver, Mr. Happy. He began to tell him the message of salvation. Mr. Happy believed and Yimso led him in the sinner's prayer. Mr. Happy confessed Jesus as his Lord and then told us how he felt different in his heart. He even came upstairs to the apartment with us after we reached New Delhi and shared some refreshments and allowed us to share with Him even more about Jesus. This definitely would not have happened had I been sitting in the front seat because I do not speak Hindi. When we reached New Delhi, I was bearing in my body the painful marks of having to lay on top of the luggage in the back seat for five hours, but I would have to say it was worth it for the soul of Mr. Happy.

HAPPENINGS IN AMRITSAR

YEAR: 2005

It seems in India we are always getting up early to catch a train. Getting up very early is not my favorite thing to do, but neither is going to the train station. On this day we were unable to purchase seats in the regular class car that we always ride in. We had to pay a little extra money to ride in the first class train car and boy was I amazed at the difference in class. We had carpeted floor, comfortable, padded seats and lots of leg room. We were traveling to a place called Amritsar which is on the border that India shares with Pakistan. It was a comfortable trip to Amritsar and when we arrived at the Pastor's house we were greeted with a welcoming party who placed garlands of marigolds around our necks. The older gentleman, who was the Pastor we were staying with, took a second wreath in his hand, came and placed it around my neck and said, "I honor you." I was shocked, partly because we had never met before, and partly because I was one of the youngest in our traveling party. After a time of meeting and greeting each other we all went inside the house. I simply sat down in the middle of the couch between two ladies I had traveled with. The Pastor looked at me and again said, "You are sitting in the middle. God honors you just as I did." At this point, I had not said anything to this kind, old Pastor except for a hello when we met at the train station. I do not know why he chose to honor me, but it made me feel special.

We had special services in Amritsar with our new friends. After the morning service, two girls came to me and begged me to come with them to their house. It felt strange without the elder ladies, but I walked with the two girls a few streets over to meet with their family. They served wonderful refreshments to me. They begged me to eat a second pastry, which are made with flaky dough. These pastries stick to your mouth and just in general make a mess. I felt rather embarrassed as they were all sitting there watching me eat their refreshments. It was a large family that I was visiting with. They kept bringing another member in one at a time to see us. When we were about to leave the mother asked us to wait just a few more minutes. She went out of the room. When she came back she placed fifty rupees in my hand, which is the equivalent of approximately one dollar. I felt humbled to see so little given with such a huge heart. I had to choke back the tears as I stood to pray for the family.

After that experience, we walked back to the Pastor's house where they had new Punjabi suits waiting for us. A Punjabi suit is the name of the clothing that the Indian women wear. As we were looking at our new suits, the Pastor brought in a tray of glasses filled with the most unusual colored beverage. It was the deepest colored reddish, purple juice I have ever seen. Fortunately the Pastor left the tray of juice for us and left the room, because it would have been embarrassing for him to see the face we all made as we tasted it. It was the saltiest, most horrible thing I have ever tasted! I had to take a deep breath and down it. It is not often that I drink something that tastes horrible and THEN ask, "What was THAT?!" Only on the mission field, I say.

    I began this chapter by talking about the honor that the Pastor chose to bestow on me. Well, after drinking the horrible juice, the Pastor chose to honor me again. After a few minutes he came back into the room with yet another glass of thick, red, salty juice. He came to me and asked me to take a drink from his glass before he did as an honor to him. I looked at the others in the room who also drank the previous glasses of juice and knew how it tasted. They were simply shrugging at me and stifling laughter. I could not refuse the old Pastor because he had been so kind to me. I took a sip, but it was a VERY SMALL sip. He told me later that I was not "sweet or sweeter, but the sweetest!" These were just a few of our happenings in Amritsar.

Church in the Slums

YEAR: 2005

It is debatable as to whether the city of New Delhi is the largest or the second largest in the world. It is such a large city that the census cannot be accurately taken. There have, without a doubt, been many improvements to the city over the years. However, there are parts of New Delhi that I discovered that are not too wonderful. These areas are called "slums." The slums are the areas where the poorest of India live. It is where many of the "untouchables" live. "The Untouchables" are the lowest of the caste system in India. Toward the end of my first trip to India, a local pastor in New Delhi wanted to take us to his church in the slums. To be perfectly honest, I was not exactly thrilled when I found out we were going into the slums, but later I was thrilled to have been there. We pulled up in a small van into the middle of the slums. Immediately, we had little faces plastered to the window of the van with their mothers standing behind them looking in as well. They were beautiful people with beautiful smiles who had simply had been born into poor families. We walked across a gravel path to a simple building with no electricity.

It was kid's club night in the slum church. I looked inside the little room to see approximately thirty young children sitting on the floor waiting for their American guests. I sang the Hindi songs I had learned and told them, through our interpreter, the Bible story about the little boy who brought his lunch to Jesus. I told them how they were never too young and never had too little for God to use their lives. After the service I sat on the floor in the middle of all the little kids posing for pictures with them, which they all loved. We were only there forty-five minutes but they were precious minutes. As we were about to leave the slums the pastor began to pass out small pieces of individually wrapped candy. One beautiful little girl, likely nine years old, had been in the service and heard the story I told them about nothing being too small for God to use. She lovingly took the piece of candy that the pastor had just given to her and held it out to me like she was offering a great treasure. I did not want to take it and told her repeatedly to keep it but she continued to offer it to me. I finally took it, knowing that she had given me something that was special to her. It was something that she did not often get. That one piece of candy is something I will never forget. A piece of candy from a child in the slums of New Delhi became one of the greatest offerings I have ever received.

THONGPE'S MIRACLE

MAY, 2005

I was back in Nagaland on the far eastern side of India. Nagaland had become a place that I loved with all my heart. The people were so beautiful and full of hospitality. Music seemed to be in their very bones. One of the staff girls from the Bible School in Dimapur had become a great friend to me. Her name was Thongpe. Since she was only a few years older than I, we spent several hours together sharing what was in our hearts. I found out on this particular night of talking with her that she had some kind of growth in her stomach which made it difficult for her to eat and sometimes breathe. Just by sitting and looking at Thongpe I felt challenged. She made me realize how short and precious life is.

Thongpe shared her heart with me. I had tears rolling down my face as I listened to her say she was afraid that she would die young. People had even told her that they saw visions of her dying young. I could not imagine the struggle that she must have had in her mind. She said, "I would feel happy to go home to God, but I don't feel satisfied with the work I have done for Him here on Earth. I want to have enough strength to cross the mountains and go to the souls who have never heard the Gospel." I felt challenged and almost stunned as I listened to my sweet, frail friend.

A few hours after sharing that time with Thongpe, something happened that changed me forever. Thongpe was outside talking with her young cousin and I was outside in a different area talking to Yimso, the Bible School director. I suddenly heard a commotion and saw the little cousin come running to get Yimso. A few minutes later, Yimso came back carrying Thongpe. She was lifeless. I took off running to get another lady and we all ran back to Thongpe's room where she was lying on the bed. Death was in the room. I had seen it earlier that afternoon on Thongpe's countenance. She was not breathing. The staff was calling out her name and shaking her but there was no life in Thongpe. We were praying. Praying in the Spirit and calling on the Giver of all life! After what seemed like an eternity, Thongpe gasped for breath. She began wheezing, but never regained consciousness. Yimso decided to take her to the hospital so they could re-hydrate her body. I was so shaken by what had just happened that there was no way I could sleep. While waiting for them to return from the hospital, I went to my room to pray. I picked up my Bible and it fell open to Mark chapter 5. My eyes immediately fell on the words, "Why make ye this ado and weep? The damsel is not dead, but sleepeth." A few hours later, I heard the vehicle pull up into the yard. What an amazing feeling to see Thongpe come walking around the corner on her own two feet!

The following night we had a foot washing service in the outside courtyard of the Bible School. This night turned out to be one of the most beautiful experiences of my life. The two older ladies washed feet on one side of the courtyard, while I and another young lady were on the other side. I had washed most of the girl's feet, almost more so with my tears than with the bucket of water. All of the sudden, I turned around to one of the girls and said, "Bring Thongpe to me! I want to wash her feet!" They told me that her feet had already been washed on the other side of the courtyard. I told them that I didn't care and I wanted them to bring her to me anyway. They brought Thongpe. I wept deeply as I washed her feet and began to pray for complete healing to her frail body. Thongpe was weeping as well. As I hugged her, it seemed to me as though she was having hard time breathing because she was crying so hard. As we wept and prayed together I began to command her healing. "Breathe!" I said. "I command your body to breathe and be well in the name of the Lord Jesus Christ!" She began to shake and breathe more deeply than she had in a long time. We both felt it the moment her healing came and we began to laugh as we hugged each other. We rejoiced together for a long time. Everyone began to tell her that her face looked completely different. Death was no longer there, but the Peace of God now reigned.

    Thongpe told me later that she had waited all day for that service to begin. She kept asking people what time it was because she was impatiently waiting for the foot washing to begin. I had told her the night as we talked that she could be healed in the anointing and foot washing service, so that is where her faith had risen to. God met us at the point of our faith. Although, He HAD already raised her from the dead! Thongpe said she kept praying that she would be brought over to me so I could wash her feet, but instead she was taken to the other side of the courtyard. She said after they washed her feet, she went back to her seat and felt disappointed. It was then that her friend came saying that I was calling for her to come to me. Thongpe said, "YOU didn't call for me. Jesus did. I have been waiting my entire life for this night. I've been waiting for you. My mother used to take me to healing crusades, but my healing never came. All my life I have been waiting for this twenty year old girl, which I did not know, to come from America. God brought you all the way from America to Nagaland for this night to happen!" I wept much at the goodness of God. To think that God would use my life in such a way is humbling. That night was a milestone in my life. Since that time, Thongpe has married and had children and lived a full life. To God be the Glory!

ONE IS NOT ENOUGH!

JULY, 2005

I had completed my first mission trip. After spending two and one-half, life-changing months in India, I did not know what to do next. There were a countless number of men and women of God who had prophesied and prayed over my life while in India. The things that they prophesied seemed like nearly impossible things to me. Every one of these men and women of God had been speaking nearly the exact same words to me without knowing what others had said. It truly amazed me each time.

After coming home from India on June 1, 2005, I went to a church service in North Little Rock, Arkansas. Pastor Charles Barnes had been one of those men who had prophesied to me about going to the nations two years before I knew that God was calling me. I went to Pastor Barnes church on July 20, 2005. That evening Pastor Barnes prayed for me and once again began to prophesy. This time his words were, "One nation is not enough, but you already know that." He spoke about me seeing the hunger that this world has for God and that I would never be able to get away from it. He spoke about going to nations not only physically, but also through prayer and intercession. "Just ask and God will do it," he said, "There is healing in your hands. What you have seen is just the beginning."

As a young woman seeking for God's direction, this was exactly what I needed to hear. I did not know it yet but I had just completed my first of a countless number of trips overseas. In the fall of that same year, I would find myself back in the nation of India once again.

THE BABY

OCTOBER, 2005

India brings new experiences each time we travel there. The spiritual world is vast because of all the idol worship and witchcraft that goes on twenty four hours a day, seven days a week. It is something that most Americans do not understand. In fact, the majority of Americans do not know the kind of lives people around the world live. Every time I go into third world countries I see something different that breaks my heart.

One such instance took place on my second trip to India. Mama Loretta and I went to the market to buy white scarves and handkerchiefs as gifts for the students of the Bible School. We went into a small shop and sat down on a bench. In a few moments two men came into the store carrying a small baby. These two men were dressed as women. In India, such men are called eunuchs. There are large colonies where these eunuchs live. The people of India are afraid of them because they operate in witchcraft. Many will quickly give money when they ask for it because of fear that the eunuchs will place a curse on them if they do not.

Into the store walked these two eunuchs carrying a baby. Because the store was so small, they were standing directly in front of us when they came in. The baby in the arms of one of the men seemed to be in a trance. It was frozen in an un-natural state. The baby's little eyes were wide open without blinking. Everything in its life was contrary to the plan of God. The men had come into the store to ask for money from the cashier. As they stood there in front of us, our hearts went out to that innocent baby. We were filled with grief at this desperate situation. Without thinking I reached out and touched the baby's hand. Instantly, the baby's hand clasped around mine and its eyes darted toward us. This was the first movement from the baby since they had come into the store, which is unnatural in itself for such a small child.

Upon receiving what they had come into the store for, the men quickly turned and left. Everything within me wanted to run after them and take that baby out of their unholy control. I even asked the pastor's wife if there was anything that we could do. She said that many times babies are given as offerings to the eunuchs to try to appease the idol gods of India. It was such a heartbreaking moment for us because we knew that this innocent child would be raised to think that the lifestyle of these men was simply normal. From that day until this, our hearts are grieved with the knowledge that centuries of idolatry has created people who are without God and past feeling. They are living in total darkness. Without end our tears are before the throne of our God concerning this.

HE NEVER SLUMBERS NOR SLEEPS

OCTOBER, 2005, WRITTEN FROM THE PERSPECTIVE OF DR. LORETTA RHOADS, OTHERWISE KNOWN AS "MAMA LORETTA."

(Dr. Rhoads) The date was set. Dozens of people in India as well as the States were laboring. There were ministers from both countries preparing. Letters had been sent. Telephone calls had been made, and now it was time. Three hundred pastors in India had come for this conference and finding a location big enough that was acceptable with the government had cost many hours on our face and on our feet. The only location in the city of Ambala was a large Catholic church. We pray that God has somehow brought increase to them for their kindness toward us. Everything went so well. The building was packed. The singing was vibrant. God was with us.

Oh how God opened up the heavens on us! People who needed renewing and new strength and the fellowship of their brethren had received it. It seemed almost impossible that this could happen in India, where Christians have much difficulty in locating a place and a date. The plans were huge to bring that many pastors for that many days. It seemed like an appointed time. Day after day we had services, teaching, and small groups. Then at night, everyone came together. The family that took us back and forth to the services had a very late night since supper always came after the evening service. Every night, dozens would come for healing. It seemed everyone was in sync. It was going well. Day one, day two, and day three we came back to the beautiful home where we were guests. Another minister and his wife from the States were with us. We had such a wonderful time in fellowship and food with Paul and Juliana, our gracious hosts. Then, it was almost midnight and time to say goodnight.

I woke up at 3:00 a.m. Suddenly, it was as though I had been wakened, but I did not know why. At the same time, I knew there was an urgent need. I closed my eyes and fell back to sleep. I have regretted that so many times. When I opened my eyes again it was 3:30 a.m. I took my Bible and went into the living room and knelt beside the chair. My prayers began with thanksgiving for my husband, David, and for the services. I lost track of the time and another minister came into the room not knowing I was there. I excused myself from the room and stepped outside knowing that I could call my husband for a little while in the early hours of the morning. In Arkansas, it was around 7:00 in the evening. My husband was traveling in his Dodge truck, pulling a trailer to pick up a load of furniture in Mississippi. We talked about our grandkids and ball games. Suddenly, my husband said, "There is so much smoke in the median," and then I lost him. I heard a screeching sound that terrified me. I began calling, "DAVID! DAVID! DAVID!"

I went back into the house and told Brother Glenn and the others that I was afraid something terrible had happened. I related to them what had just transpired and then I began to make phone calls. I located the head of the State police who was a relative of our best friends, the Thompsons. I also contacted our family doctor. I did not know all that happened, but I did find out that there had been a terrible wreck, and that David had been air-lifted to the Trauma hospital in Memphis, Tennessee. They went ahead and held morning services of the conference, but Melissa and I packed our things into a car. The pastors and ministers gathered around us and prayed for us and for David even though we were all still in a fog of what had actually taken place. Melissa and I began the five hour drive toward New Delhi to fly home. Melissa never said a word the entire time. She simply was there with me and held my hand.

This is when time stops and we are waiting for the voice on the other end of the phone that says, "All is well." We began our silent journey toward New Delhi not knowing what was transpiring at home. David had actually been placed on the side of the highway and covered up with a sheet and called dead, but then someone saw the sheet move. That is when they air lifted him to the hospital. The driver in the truck behind David had been killed. There were nine tractor trailers, David's truck and trailer and one car involved in a massive pile up due to the black smoke that had covered the interstate. When David came to, he was inside of an MRI machine not knowing what had happened to him. He began to move, and then heard a voice telling him to be still while they ran a test. With his never-ending wit, David said, "Do you mind telling me what kind of test we are running?"

They told David that his neck was broken, but he began to move his neck back and forth telling them that his neck was NOT broken. About two and a half hours into our trek toward New Delhi, we finally received a phone call from my son-in-law with a message from David. The message was that David was fine and he DID NOT want us to abandon our mission before it was finished. David's truck had been completely demolished. His truck had gone under the semi that had crossed in front of him after going into the black smoke. His message to me was, "Do not come home! If you had been here, you would not be alive, because the seat that you would have been sitting in is no longer there. You are where you are supposed to be!"

David did not tell me the extent of his injuries until after I arrived home from India nearly a week and a half later. He could not remember our conversation that we had been having when the wreck happened. He could not figure out how I knew what was going on all the way over in India. The truth is I was the one who alerted the police and my family that something was wrong, all the way from India. David had sustained a severe head injury in the wreck and had to bear one-hundred and twenty-five stitches on the left side of his head. All of which, he did not tell me until I returned home simply because he wanted me to finish what God had sent us to India to do. That is David's heart. Miraculously, just shy of two weeks after this horrific incident, David, along with Melissa's parents, met us at the Tulsa airport. We were absolutely amazed that he looked perfectly normal. We could not see a bruise. We could not see a stitch, but we did shed a lot of tears and still do to this day at the miraculous hand of God.

    Our catastrophes and disappointments are not new to our God who knew it all from the beginning. He never slumbers. He never sleeps. I've tried to say thank you the way humans do when they are overwhelmed with love and gratitude. I remain amazed at what

God did. My husband, David, has gone on since that wreck to continue working in the nations of the world as he has always loved to do. He even returned to India with us a year and a half later to preach and build the roof on a home for widows in far Eastern India.

What do you sing after the wreck? What do you sing after the catastrophe that came out of nowhere? What do you sing when your peace has been shattered? What song could possibly sum up the sentiments of your heart? I do not know what you sing, but the song that we choose to sing is, "I'm going on. I'm going on. I'm going on toward the mark, toward the goal. So many lives depend on what I do. Give me the strength, Dear Lord, I'm going on for You."

No Better Place

NOVEMBER 2005

We traveled to the border of India and Pakistan where Pastor John was the overseer of fifty village churches. He took us to the changing of the guard that takes places at the border every day. It is a big fanfare and lots of spectators go to watch. Loretta and I were seated roughly five feet from the Pakistan border. There was a big soldier with a big gun standing there on the line between the two nations. I was tempted to just stick my foot across the line to say I had been in Pakistan, but I did not want to challenge the authority of that guard. I looked across the line to where three Pakistani, Muslim women were seated. All three of them were dressed in the full black burka. Seeing them really grabbed my heart because I had just finished reading a book titled, "The Torn Veil," in which a Muslim woman tells her story of how Jesus appeared to her, told her who He was, healed her body and set her free. I must say it felt surreal sitting there surrounded by those people.

From there, Pastor John took us to one of the village churches. It was close to the border and very remote. Pastor John told us how the Christians in the village have to deal with questions from the police all the time and are blamed for things that are not their fault. We entered the village with this knowledge, praying that God would help us encourage these brothers and sisters. The people were very poor. All the children came running when we arrived. I had fun taking pictures, asking their names, playing patty-cake, making faces and singing to them. During the service that evening I was sitting on an uncomfortable rope cot. The circulation in my legs was being cut off behind my knees because my feet did not reach the ground. Smoke was wafting up from the cooking fire into my face and causing me to cough and my back was hurting from not having anything to lean against for a long period of time. In the middle of all of that I had this thought:

"Dear Jesus, isn't it amazing that with all the comforts I have at home and all the places I could go, there is no place on earth I would rather be than right here, right now in this dirty, poor, border village."

As I looked at those people, I truly had gratefulness in my heart to be able to share Jesus with them.

The Long Day

NOVEMBER, 2005

We were traveling to a place in India we had never been to before. It was close to the India/Pakistan border. This place is called Ferozepur. In India, you must learn that punctuality is quite literally a foreign concept. There were three of us traveling together and we were already quite tired from several long days and nights of hard travel. After arriving in Ferozepur, we were told that we would be leaving the next morning at 7:30 a.m. and travel for two and one-half hours to a conference where we would be ministering. In spite of being exhausted, we awoke at 6:30 and got ourselves ready to leave on time. However, our hosts were not ready to leave until 10:00 a.m. I must honestly say that physical weariness generally does not bring out the best in us. We were somewhat frustrated about the lack of time management. It is not good to be frustrated when you have a long day of ministry ahead of you.

We finally crammed, (and I do literally mean crammed), into an SUV and headed out for the conference. I sang in the Hindi language that morning and had a new experience with the Indian culture. I had not yet experienced that when they like a person who is singing they will bring money up onto the stage. While holding it in their hands, they will circle it above the head of the one singing and then lay it at their feet. I suppose they feel it will bring blessings on them. So, this began to happen to me. One after another would come up onto the stage with me, circle money around my head and then lay it on the floor. I must say it was quite an interesting experience for me!

We were ministering outside under a colorful tent in very hot weather. The people were gracious and brought beautiful colored wreaths and placed them around our necks. Mama Loretta happened to be wearing a white blouse that day. At the end of the day, however, her blouse was no longer only white, but had blue and red and yellow spots all over it from the dye that was in the wreaths. We thought it was humorous.

After ministering there all day long, we left and headed back toward Ferozepur where we were to be at another meeting scheduled for 8:30 that evening. Along the way we stopped at a pastor's home for a restroom and the afternoon chai (tea). During our stop, a family called the pastor on the telephone, desperately requesting prayer for a family member. The pastor asked Mama Loretta to pray in English and he would interpret to the family on the phone. Mama Loretta, being a mighty prayer warrior, began to pray with the pastor interpreting. After a minute or so, Mama Loretta began to pray in the tongues of the Holy Ghost and the pastor continued to interpret to the family. I was standing off to the side but immediately noticed what was happening. When they finished praying, the pastor was weeping and told us, "I knew you were praying in the Spirit, but I also knew exactly what you were saying. I've never had that happen before!" The Bible tells us in I Corinthians 12 that there are "tongues, and interpretation of tongues," which are the gifts of the Holy Ghost. We saw that in full operation that day.

After finishing the un-expected prayer meeting, we knew we were too late for the next meeting. Thinking that we were headed back to the pastor's house in Ferozepur, we piled into the SUV and tried to relax. The next thing we heard was the pastor's wife answering her telephone. The phone call was from the pastor who said that people were still waiting on us to come and minister to them. It was now 10:00 p.m. We all thought to ourselves, "You've got to be kidding me?!" To tell the truth, none of us were excited about this news. We were past exhaustion.

We decided to go ahead to the next meeting because we felt bad that people were still waiting on us after such a long delay. A few minutes past 10:00 p.m. we arrived for the church service. It was cool in the evenings there. We walked in the dark, with only the moon lighting our path. Literally, we were walking on heaps of trash to reach the meeting place. We walked into a courtyard where people were seated on the hard ground. They were all wrapped up in blankets. We found out that the people had been waiting on us for hours. Once again, our exhaustion changed into compassion and our prayer became, "Lord, do not let us fail these precious people." Through tears we sang and preached the Gospel of Jesus Christ which is the power for salvation. In the minutes that followed, we were rewarded with the raising of hands and prayers of repentance in response to God's Word. The words of Paul the Apostle was in our hearts. "How can they believe on whom they have not heard, and how can they hear without a preacher." Two hours later, with weary bodies, we began our final journey to a place of rest for the night, but our spirits were soaring! This is the reason we came! This is the call that we responded to as we wept in surrender to God's Will. The people who sat in darkness saw a great light that night in the church built around the trash dump. Never had a church looked more beautiful than under the canopy of God's starry skies. We left well after midnight and completely exhausted, but we left there with our ears filled with the rejoicing sounds of new Believers.

So Many Delays!

MARCH, 2006

Once again we were headed to Nagaland which required government permits to enter, and once again, we could not get these permits because we only had a group of three people. We headed out anyway with a plan of how we were going to reach the Bible School. To initially get there required us to take an hour and a half flight to Guwahati, and then head to a train station to ride for another six hours. However, this particular trip didn't work out that smoothly. Our flight was uneventful, but upon landing we discovered that one of our suitcases did not make it on the flight. We had to stay and wait on the suitcase because it contained important items that we were taking to the Bible School. We ended up staying the night in the airport and picked our suitcase up the next morning. With that behind us, we headed to the train station where we discovered that our train was delayed. This was not really an unusual event because the trains are late many times in India. So, we waited for hours, but our train did not arrive. We noticed that there 'just so happened' to be another train sitting in the station going to the same place we were headed, and it 'just so happened' that a group of fifty people did not show up for the train. We were able to switch our tickets over to the second train and board it with about three minutes to spare before it pulled out. Finally, we were on our way after so many delays!

    After five hours we got off the train at a little spot in the road and into a vehicle. We rode for three hours over roads that I cannot even describe to you. Our vehicle could have nearly been lost in some of the potholes. We knew we were headed to a police check point and were not sure what the outcome would be since we had no permits. However, because of all the delays we had experienced, we did not reach the police check point until 3:00 a.m. We began to hide under blankets and scarves in the back seat and try to appear as though we were asleep with our heads covered. We slowly pulled up to the check point, but no one was there. They were all asleep inside the building. Our driver honked the horn several times until one of the officers came stumbling outside, simply rolled the gate back and waved us through!

OUT OF WEAKNESS

April, 2006

The mission field many times requires long days of tiring travel. One such day we traveled early in the morning from New Delhi to Ambala City, which was about a three hour trip. We then immediately left with the Pastor, his wife and son and traveled another hour to a village church. There, we found fifty people packed into an extremely small room. We began to minister to them through singing and the Word. There was a mother sitting directly in front of me with a small girl on her lap. There were so many people in such a small room that the child was practically laying on my feet. The child was moaning and out of her head with fever. I knelt down and prayed for the child. We traveled on from there to other villages sharing the Gospel and praying. We saw many come to the Lord.

Almost two weeks later, during the Passover Celebration we were hosting in Ambala City, I began to feel dizzy. I went upstairs while the other ladies continued to pray for people. When they came up the stairs later in the evening they found me shivering under heavy blankets in spite of the ninety degree temperature. By the next day, Pastor Prakash was concerned about our further travel into more remote areas. He recommended that I be taken to New Delhi where I could receive medical attention if needed. They were alarmed at first that I might have contracted malaria or some type of communicable disease. Richard and Sally Melin, a medical doctor and RN, came from their travels in Indonesia to New Delhi just in time to give us medical advice. Doctor Melin said immediately that I was extremely dehydrated. I had been running a temperature of 104 and 105 for several days. They bought supplies for us in the market and then left for services they were scheduled to be in on the Pakistan border. Within a few hours after they left I began to see a red rash appear all over my body. Mama Loretta called for a taxi and we headed for Apollo Hospital in New Delhi. Upon seeing me walk in, they sent me immediately to the Emergency Room and began trying to find a vein where they could hydrate me through an IV. There were several doctors around my bed asking questions, but I was nearly out of my head with fever. The doctors and nurses there gave me excellent care. They took appropriate samples for lab studies, and within forty-eight hours I learned that I had German measles. After learning this we requested that I be given proper medication and be allowed to return to the apartment where we were staying.

In the week that followed I was a very sick and weak young woman. Mama Loretta was with me every moment, caring for me. There is one moment in all of it that stands out clearly to me. On one of those days, I tried to get up out of the bed to head to the restroom. Mama Loretta came into the room and saw me holding on to the wall. She came over and wrapped her arms around me to hold me up. I laid my head on her shoulder and said, "Mama, am I going to die?"

"No! You are NOT going to die," was Mama Loretta's firm reply.

There were people praying for me all over the world. Word had spread to people in Indonesia, Nepal, all over India, and all over the United States. People I had never met had been given the news to pray for me in India. God hears prayers, and He knows my name. At the age of twenty-one, I recovered from the measles. We concluded later that I contracted them from the little girl in the village who was so sick. Instead of frightening me about returning to the mission field, the entire experience gave me peace in knowing that God will bring you through difficult, painful and trying experiences. I can honestly say, though not in my physical body, that experience made me stronger.

Romans 8:28 says, "For we know that all things work together for the good of them that love God, to them who are the called according to his purpose." That's enough for me.

OH THE BLOOD OF JESUS!

YEAR: 2006

We got up at 5:30 in the morning to be able to reach the train station in Ambala, India, by 7:00 a.m. to purchase train tickets to New Delhi. We typically bought our tickets prior to reaching the train station, but on this occasion, we did not have that option. Upon reaching the train station, we discovered that there were no seats to be had on the train we needed. We purchased tickets for a later train and then stood in the station for over an hour while everyone stared at us. There was a group of four men standing nearby and I felt that they were up to no good. I prayed under my breath until they finally left.

A little while later, we heard a woman screaming across the station. We were looking to see what was going on when we realized she was screaming at us! We had not done anything except stand in one spot. We knew immediately that she was demon possessed. She was approximately 50 feet from where we were screaming loudly and being obnoxious. It was obvious to everyone in the station that she was screaming at the group of white people. Pastor Prakash, our host in India, began to interpret to us that she was telling everyone in the station who we were and what we were there to do. Graceson, Pastor Prakash's son, said that she was trying to curse us. We all put our luggage in the middle and made a circle around it. We began to pray in our circle and to softly sing about the blood of Jesus. I began to sing, "Satan the blood of Jesus is against you, and God will give us the victory!" The demon possessed woman could not hear us, as she was too far away, but it was only a few short moments until she sat down and shut her mouth.

NO LANGUAGE BARRIER

YEAR: 2006

I have been awed by a common factor in every country I have traveled in. At times, when I sing in English, people begin to weep. This has amazed me because very few people understand English in the places we have been. This was especially true in China, where no one understood English. I would sing the song,

"Lord, I want to love you more

than I ever have before.

You're so easy to adore.

Lord I want to love you more."

Many tears were shed with our brothers and sisters in that country. I would weep when they would sing, and they wept when I sang. How is this possible? It is because the Spirit of God has NO LANGUAGE BARRIER. We are different members of the Body of Christ, from different parts of the world, but we are of the SAME SPIRIT.

    On one of my trips we travelled to a Bible School in the far Eastern region of India. We met some precious students who had come from the country of Burma to study. These students did not know a word of English and I certainly didn't know the Burmese language. One afternoon, we were together in the church singing. The Burmese students sang a beautiful song in their language. I couldn't stop the fountain of tears from flowing. It was an incredible and new experience for me. I somehow managed to ask them to sing it again several days later and the same thing happened. The tears were un-stoppable. I persistently asked around until I found an Indian student who understood some Burmese. "PLEASE, tell me what the meaning of that song is," I pleaded. I was amazed at what I heard next. The student told me that the song was a story about a missionary who went to Burma with the Gospel of Christ. It was all about his struggles, and it was his declaration that no matter how hard it got, he would do whatever it took to continue preaching about Jesus. I suddenly understood why I was weeping every time I heard the song. The Spirit of God that lives in me understood perfectly even though my natural mind didn't. An amazing truth that I have learned is that there are no barriers to the Spirit of God.

When Jesus Comes

YEAR: 2007

"When Jesus comes, the tempter's power is broken. When Jesus comes, all fears are wiped away. He takes the gloom and fills the life with glory. For all is changed, when Jesus comes to stay." These are the lyrics to an old song.

We were high in the mountains of Far Eastern India. So high, in fact, that no foreigners ever go there. So high, that we were looking DOWN on clouds. It took us SIXTEEN HOURS in a vehicle to travel approximately 200 miles. The roads were worse than terrible and it was curve after curve after curve. The terrain was straight up the mountain on one side of the road and sheer cliffs on the other side with no barriers to prevent us from going over the side. We passed places where memorials had been set up for buses that went off the side of the mountain with no survivors. This was the greatest test of endurance I had ever faced. Sixteen hours in ANY car is a long time, but in those conditions is was even longer. There were no bathrooms available except for the bushes and no places to stop for food.

We finally arrived at Shamator and began to hold services in a large church building on top of the mountain. The people, however, were not responding to our altar calls. We would tell them, "We want to pray with you. We want to pray for your sick bodies. Please come!" No one would come. For one thing, they were shy. Secondly, we were foreigners. Thirdly, they were used to praying at their seats, not going forward for prayer. We were struggling with this because of the difficulty it had taken us to reach them and we wanted to do what we had been sent by God to do.

I was to preach on our second afternoon there. The only thing I had in my heart were the words to the old song, "When Jesus Comes," so I sang the song. I was amazed as the back of the church filled with people coming in from the outside when I began to sing. I then began to preach, "When Jesus Comes, EVERYTHING CHANGES!" I told them how deaf people came to Jesus and EVERYTHING CHANGED. I preached about how the blind came to Jesus and EVERYTHING CHANGED! I preached about how Jesus passed by dead people and EVERYTHING CHANGED! I preached about how Jesus is going to come again someday and EVERYTHING IS GOING TO CHANGE!

I then began to woo the people I was preaching to. The Spirit of God had spoken to me specifically about how to ask them to come forward so we could pray for them. I did what I had been told and the PEOPLE CAME! Imagine that! They came forward with every kind of illness and need and God healed them and set them free. The

Lord had spoken to me and said, "You call the sick forward, and I will meet them and change everything!" That is just what HE did!

We all know that our God has never changed. He is the same "yesterday, today and forever!" I want to encourage you today: HE will NEVER CHANGE, but He can CHANGE EVERYTHING in the circumstances of your life. Just trust Him.

WHAT FRUSTRATION?

YEAR: 2008

In the spring of 2008 we once again went to India. On this trip Mama Loretta's husband, Brother David Rhoads, was with us and we were headed to places in South India where we had never been. The majority of our ministry had always been in North India. The trip started out on a less than glorious note. I came down with the flu the night before we left, but 3:00 a.m. the next morning we headed out. My head was spinning and my fever was high, but I was going no matter what. The fifteen hour flight to India was pure misery to put it mildly. I have, in my few short years of being a missionary, acquired a newfound admiration and respect for everything the Apostle Paul went through on his missionary journeys!

We reached India safely and within a week I was feeling better. We ministered in several different places in Vijayawada, India, before being told that we were going out to an extremely remote area. "It will take us approximately an hour and a half to reach this place," said our host, "we are going to dedicate a brand new church!" We were headed out to an area where the people were steeped in witchcraft. These people are the Banjara tribal people of South India. An Indian pastor had gone into this place and started working with the people. Many had accepted Christ and come out of witchcraft. They had constructed a simple brick building that was not yet completed, but they wanted it dedicated to the Lord.

We all climbed into the van that morning excited about a brand new opportunity! Expecting to only be riding on the rough roads for an hour and a half, you can imagine the frustration that was piling up after five hours had passed and we still were not to our destination. Six hours passed by! We were all just about to the breaking point. There were no places to stop for bathrooms and there had been no food that day. It was extremely hot and we were all getting angry. I'm not saying we were right. I am just being honest about how it really was.

Finally, we pulled up in front of a clay house with a straw thatched roof, dodging the cattle as we pulled in. We were in the middle of huge fields of red chili peppers. Climbing out of the van, our frustration was still very present. The first request was for someone to please show us a restroom. This was almost a comical request, because the people scurried to find something we could use as a door on the already existing door-less outhouse. Oh my, what memories!

That detail being settled, we walked over to where a small group of people had gathered and there received some shattering news. The pastor, whom we had come to celebrate with and dedicate all of his hard work to the Lord, had been killed in a trucking accident just a couple of hours before we arrived. The family and some of the church members were still at the hospital with his body. The frustration and anger we were carrying melted away as though it had never existed and compassion took its place. We went ahead with the dedication service with the few members that were present. With love and compassion we blessed those people and prayed over the man that would take on the role of becoming the new pastor. We did our best to encourage those precious new Believers, and repented for the anger we had felt. Many tears were shed that afternoon on that rural farmland of South India. We learned that no cost is too much. We learned that it is not easy to go to the "ends of the Earth," but someone has to in order to reach those who live there.

PASHUPATI

YEAR: 2008

We were in Nepal. After flying into Kathmandu, we spent days traveling to different regions of Nepal and ministering the Gospel. The people of Nepal are so beautiful and sensitive to the Presence of God that it makes this country one my favorite places to go. That is why this particular experience will never leave my mind. We were traveling with another minister who had worked in the country of Nepal for many years. He told us that he wanted to take us to a couple of places to do a prayer walk. He said, "When we get to this place, you are going to have to make sure that you are praying continually." Nothing could have prepared me for what we were about to see, smell and experience.

When we pulled up to this place called Pashupati, I smelled an unfamiliar and repulsive stench in the air. We were praying as we walked down a long pathway. All along the path were Hindu holy men, witch doctors consulting with people, and women filled with evil spirits selling flowers to place around dead bodies. The heavy oppression was indescribable and unlike anything we had ever experienced. The place we were walking in was a stronghold of Satan. It is darkness, even in the noonday sun, that is beyond explanation. The wailing of mourners clustered around the burning bodies of their loved ones assaulted our senses. Pashupati is a place ruled by Hindu priests. It is a series of temples and platforms where dead bodies of Hindus are burned. A river runs through the middle of it but it is so polluted with filth and the ashes of dead bodies that it could hardly be called a river. Mourners wash their bodies in the filthy water thinking that they are washing away sins. Hindu priests sit around on the temple site and perform signs and wonders in the eyes of the people. This place is void of hope and light.

It is the closest thing to Hell that exists on this Earth.

    We were all praying in our hearts as we entered the gate. As we walked in, a woman turned and pointed at us and in a shrieking voice began to chatter in her language. Our interpreter told us, "That woman is telling everyone who you are and saying that you are full of light and that you do not belong here." As we continued inside, we saw four women wailing and mourning over the dead body of a man that was being prepared for burning. They were washing their arms and faces in the filthy river. The sound of their wailing still echoes in our hearts years later because it was the sound of utter despair. We ask ourselves to this day if they yet know the truth. That memory is etched forever in our hearts and minds. Sometimes people ask why we would jeopardize our lives for the sake of another? This one memory is the answer to that question. We walked away from Pashupati heartsick and with the stench of burning flesh in our nostrils. We felt sick to our stomach. How was this possible?

    Only a few minutes later we walked into another scene. This one was more deceptive that the first. The sun was shining. Streets were swept. Everything was painted white. Colorful flags were blowing in the wind. Gentle music was playing. People were walking, talking and laughing everywhere. They were twirling prayer wheels and counting prayer beads. They were seeking peace in all the wrong places. We were in the courtyard of one of the largest Buddhist temples in Nepal. Everything seemed light and beautiful compared to Pashupati. In reality, it is more dangerously deceptive.

    At the end of this day in Nepal, our hearts were so heavy with the weight of what we had seen that at midnight we were still weeping and praying together for the souls of the men and women we had witnessed. The reality still hits us to this very day that the people we saw were only a tiny representation of the millions in India and Nepal who believe those very things. That day in Nepal is not one of those beautiful memories that you like to go back and relive, but we do relive it constantly because it is the reality of how lost and deceived the people of those nations are. It is the one memory from our work on the mission field that causes us to go again and again no matter what the hardship or cost is. It is the memory that drives us to tell the lost about Jesus, the Savior. It drives us to tell them about the God of light and love, the God of peace and the God of all things holy. It drives us because it gave us a glimpse of what an eternity in Hell will be like for the souls who do not know God. Jesus was moved with compassion as He saw people without hope. We must likewise let compassion rise in our hearts for the souls who do not live in the reality of God's love.

One year later, we found ourselves back in Kathmandu just a few miles from Pashupati. We were with a group of three hundred Christians who had set aside three days to fast and pray. When we arrived they had already begun the prayer meeting and had been fasting with water only. I was chosen to speak first to the assembly. I had nothing prepared, but as I reached the platform I remembered the experience of Pashupati the year before. I began to preach about "A Sound." I spoke to them concerning the sounds that we heard going on in Pashupati, sounds of hopelessness. I challenged them to raise their voices to the heavens and let a sound be heard, a sound of hope, a sound of righteousness, a sound of praise and intercession to the living God. Up until this time, the people had been quietly praying. There had not been a real breakthrough in prayer. That day, however, when they realized that the kingdom of darkness was not afraid to lift its voice, those precious saints of Nepal lifted their voice like a mighty army. The sound of the rushing mighty wind was all around us. For over two hours we prayed and cried out to God without a break for the souls of Nepal.

    Since that time, there have been dozens of village churches raised up in Nepal. The pastors of these churches walk for hours any given week to share the message of God's love. Some of the pastors that we have had the privilege to work with lead multiple gatherings of Believers. Some have buildings but most worship outside or in homes. The last time we saw three of these pastors, they had shoes that were falling apart and shirts with holes in them. Day after day, they would wear the same shirt to the conference where they had come to meet with us. We have had the privilege of dedicating some of the new churches filled with Believers these pastors have won to the Lord. Yes, Pashupati exists in Nepal, but we left there knowing that the darkness had been penetrated by the Light of the world.

FACES!

(THE NATION OF CHINA)

(WRITTEN FROM THE PERSPECTIVE OF DR. LORETTA RHOADS)

(Dr. Rhoads) People were not sipping coffee or drinking tea. They were not talking and laughing with one another. The furnishings did not matter. I walked in. I heard a voice. I saw faces. Every one of them was there on purpose. They did not come to tell funny stories. They were looking for someone who could bring meaning to this existence because they look death in the face every day. Little wonder that they are deeper in God than the average American who can get up and walk out of church with a cup in their hand and decide they have had enough. God's got a people. If you look at their faces, you know...

Pastors are pastoring thousands secretly by going into homes and alleys and wooded areas. We spend billions on building "churches" and many of them are empty, certainly empty of God. Whereas other faces are climbing up dark steps thinking, 'Where will it be this time?' Little wonder that they know the secrets of God. They live in a secret place.

There will be a morning for the nation of China. It may be that more Christians will die in China this year than any other nation. They are persecuted and killed, but told us personally, "Do not pray for persecution to stop. It shows who the true Christians are." They get out of prison, released in the morning, and then run and seek after another secret place so they may know the depth and secrets of our God. Many times they tear one page out of a Bible from someone else because they do not have one of their own, and then memorize every word. I cannot condemn this nation of America. I live here. I like the ease of getting into a vehicle and going where I want to, going to the "church." The American church loves to sip coffee and tell stories. We are entertained while God's heart is broken. The "church" for the most part has ceased to be.

Ezekiel, the prophet, was called out to a bone yard. Everywhere he looked it was just bones. Once there had been life. Sometimes we wonder if the framework, the bones, is even left in the American church. The American church touts what they "use to do." The Chinese church lives it now. The American church, however, acts like a wisp in the wind. I read in my Bible and find words like "thunder and lightning." Words that speak of the atmosphere changing! How long has it been, Mr. and Ms. America, since we let God use us to change the atmosphere? There is a place, a secret place, in God. We've become so distracted, so attached to the latest and newest thing.

I fall on my face, trembling, like Daniel and Ezekiel. I read these two books again and again. They found the place where a man from another world greeted them; A secret place. I found that place. I do not know how long the prayer lasted. One lady said they had been sitting there for more than an hour listening to me. I was amazed that the group was all sitting quietly when I came to myself. One dear sister, Dianne Isaacs, came over to me and said, "Where have you been? You have been speaking the Chinese language." We had formed a circle to have just one more prayer that Saturday afternoon in that beautiful room. We had been blessed with a wonderful meal and had been praying and fellowshipping together most of the day. I was not anticipating this experience. I was not thinking of China. I had never been to China. As we joined hands for that final prayer, I was caught up in a vision. I saw a Chinese woman, standing in a field with a pointed hat of a field laborer. She was bent, weary from the labor. I watched as she began beckoning to me to come and help her. I was completely consumed with what I was seeing and for the next window of time was lost in the Spirit. Four years later, through a Divine connection, I trembled with tears rolling down my face as I exited the airport in Beijing, China. As my feet stepped out of that airport and on to Chinese soil, all I could think of was that woman who beckoned me to come years before. I knew I was walking in the steps the Master had ordained.

There is more than one standing on Chinese soil, beckoning, calling out for help. That day I was lost to a voice from another world. That voice came out of my mouth and then took my feet years later to that place of beckoning. Many times people brush these things aside calling it weird, but God is saying all the time, "Where Is my son and my daughter who are listening for the sound of the Beloved? Where are those that are reaching for My hand?"

How many have died? They told us it was in the millions for the sake of the Gospel. "Of whom the world is not worthy." They allow themselves to be lit with the flame of the Holy Ghost and then utterly consumed. We see their faces often. We see the eyes of those precious men and women of God that we prayed with, wept with and laughed with. We see that man who had his teeth knocked out in prison. We see those few that we baptized in secrecy in the ankle deep water of a bathtub. We see the tiny rooms where we had church that were packed so tightly that not one more person could fit inside. China, we weep for you. It is so easy to say we love you.

AT THE BORDER

YEAR: 2008

We were traveling inside the nation of China. Incredible things had been happening not only in our secret meetings as we traveled across the country but also in our own hearts. One day we all got into a small bus and headed north. I knew we were going to be traveling for ten hours across the countryside and I knew that we were going to be stopping in two places for ministry. However, I did not know that we were going to be staying the night across the river from North Korea. It was late that night when we checked into our hotel. I could not see much because it was so dark. As we walked to our room, I was asked if I saw that our hotel was on the bank of a river. I did. I was then told that the bank on the other side of the river was the nation of North Korea. I was shocked! No one knew that for years I had carried a burden for the nation of North Korea. No one knew that I had purchased books from the Voice of the Martyrs ministry about North Korea. No one knew how many times I had prayed and wept over the Christians who are persecuted there. Only God knew. He was the One who had given me the burden. He was the One who knew where I would be sitting that night. He was the One who had ordered my steps to this place. My heart was racing as I walked into our room for the night. I wrote in my journal with my hands shaking. My entire being was shivering, not only from the cold, but also from the reality of my situation. I could not help but think, 'How in the world did I get here?!' Of all people, it was me! Of all places, it was North Korea! Here I was sitting just across the river from a nation that is considered to be one of the most dangerous in the world. Here I was on the border of North Korea.

The next morning it was cold, foggy and dreary as we exited our hotel. I tripped and painfully twisted my ankle as we came down the steps. I knew the enemy was trying to throw a kink in my experience with God in this unlikely and amazing place. I persevered anyway. There is much that is established in you when you persevere in the place God has placed you no matter how difficult it can get. We walked to the edge of the river and looked across to the bare border of North Korea. From where we were standing there was a huge bridge extending out into the water, but it only went half way across the river. From the China border, a nice bridge jutted out across the water. However, from the North Korea side of the border, there were only broken concrete columns protruding out of the water where the other half of the bridge used to be. We found out that the bridge had been damaged in the Korean War, but it had never been rebuilt because the Korean government promotes intense propaganda against America. It is promoted so much that some in North Korea think that their nation is still at war with us. On the China side, where we were standing, there were hotels and restaurants, electricity and cars. On the North Korea side there appeared to be nothing. When we arrived the night before, it was lit up on our side of the river, but it was pitch black on the other side. I stood in awe at where I was.

    We then drove a little further to a place where you could get in a boat in the river between the two countries. We were amazed at the desolate landscape of North Korea that stretched out before us. There were a few small houses that scattered the hilly landscape, but we saw no one moving around. It began to drizzle a frigid rain as we climbed into the boat. The temperature had only reached into the thirties. Our entire purpose for driving that far was to get into that boat, float down that river, stretch our hands toward that Nation and pray. We did so standing there in the rain. Naïve to the severity of what could happen, I pulled my camera up to take some pictures. As I did our group leader said, "No, Melissa! Do not let anyone see that you are taking pictures! There is a prison on this river bank and there are rifles aimed at us right now. They will shoot if they see you because they will assume you are a foreign spy. They have shot people before and this time would be no different." I very quickly put my camera down as we continued floating down the river.

Later, I went down into the lower cabin of the boat. Fortunately there was a place for us to get out of the cold wind and rain. It was not anything fancy. There were only narrow boards running along the wall of the cabin for people to sit on. The cabin did however have some tinted, glass windows down below through which I was able to take some photos of that closed country. There were rusted, upside down boats that littered the river bank. We saw one man on a bicycle. We saw the prison. We saw the rifles. My heart still breaks to this day when I think of those precious and beautiful people living in that nation. Only through the supernatural will they ever be able to hear the truth of the Gospel. Only through the light of God will the darkness of the lies be broken from their minds, and only eternity will reveal what all happened in those moments of prayer along the river bank border of North Korea.

WATER IN THE DESERT

YEAR: 2009/2010

For many years at the Bible School compound in Ambala there was not enough water. We had to make do many days with just a five gallon bucket of water. Often times, this was during the heat of a summer day. I remember days of ministering until our clothes were soaked with sweat. We would then go upstairs to our little room to clean up but no water would come out of the faucet when turned on. We often had over one-hundred people using a small amount of water each day. The young men would make an exhausting trip on bicycles and bring back gallons of water to have enough to finish out the day. Big water tanker trucks would come during the week and fill the water tank on top of the Bible School, but it only lasted a short time. We saw, and knew first hand, the tremendous need for a constant water supply. We began to discuss options. The most obvious solution was to drill a water well.

Pastor Prakash began as soon as possible talking with local well drillers to discuss our desperate need. The men he spoke with shook their heads at the possibility of drilling a well on the Bible School property. They called it impossible because there was not a water table underground in that area. People had tried before, but to no avail. What they did not know was that Pastor Prakash is a man of great faith in God. Instead of being discouraged by their words, the Pastor asked them to come and try drilling anyway. We were not deterred by their doubt, but were actually excited about the fact that we were going to have water.

The drilling commenced. To the satisfaction of the well drilling company there was no water just as they had said. This was a bit of a discouraging thing to Pastor Prakash but nothing worth giving up over. The drilling continued for longer than expected. The men drilled deeper than they had ever drilled before and still there was no water. All was looking hopeless, equipment was breaking, and the well drillers were to the point of quitting. They told Pastor Prakash that he was wasting their time, his time and his money. It looked like it was over. It looked like we were just going to have to live with a lack of water. It looked like our faith attempt had been fruitless.

Being the man of God that he is, Pastor Prakash asked the well drillers to try just ONE MORE TIME for water. The drillers reluctantly agreed. As they began the last attempt, Pastor Prakash slipped inside the house and into his office where he has the flag of Israel hanging on the wall facing the direction of Israel. For as long as I have known him, Pastor begins praying in this manner, "God of Abraham, Isaac and Jacob," and this particular day was no different. As he stood there facing the flag of Israel, he lifted his hands toward Heaven and began to pray, "Oh God of Abraham, Isaac, and Jacob, I know that you gave water to Your people in the wilderness. Just as you gave water at the well of Be'er, I'm asking You..." Suddenly, before he could finish his prayer, there was a booming sound that filled the house. Pastor went running, along with others, to find out what caused the loud noise. When he reached the drilling point, he was met with the amazement of the well drillers. Here they had been working and drilling deeper than ever before for quite some length of time, here they had been frustrated, here they had almost given up, but SUDDENLY, there was a BOOM. They had no explanation to give. They were stunned as they told Pastor Prakash that as they were making that last attempt there was a booming noise and somehow they had hit water. In fact, they had hit an underground river that they were not aware of. We knew that the God of Abraham, Isaac and Jacob had just provided a modern day 'water in the desert' miracle.

    To this day, the Bible School does not have to be concerned with a lack of water. To this day, other households on adjoining property cannot access the same water that Pastor has privilege to. To this day we are amazed at the miracle coming out of the faucet without limits. Continuing to pray when everyone tells you that it is over can change the impossible. Pure faith when things look like they are hopeless produces the miraculous. We experience it every time we turn the faucet in Ambala, India.

TWELVE MIRACLES

SEPTEMBER, 2010

The two months that I was about to spend in India, unknown to me, were about to be some of the most miraculous and eventful days of growing and seeking the Lord I had ever experienced. We arrived at the end of September and spent a couple of days, like normal, resting because of the jet lag. The second night I awoke from a vivid dream. In the dream I was in my home church in Arkansas. I was at the front of the church praying and weeping when a man and a lady in my church came over to pray for me. The man, Bro. Jerry Faulkner, was weeping and began to pray, "Oh God, give Melissa twelve very specific miracles while she is in India this time." Upon waking up I remembered the dream and felt that God was trying to tell me that something special would take place during my time there.

That night, I preached my first message to the fifty Bible School students and titled it, "Finding God." I challenged them to be like Jacob when he said to the Angel of the Lord, "I will not let you go until you bless me." At the end of my message, I shared with them the dream about twelve miracles. The wind of the Spirit blew through that sanctuary that night in a way I had never experienced. The faith of the students rose and we saw the first miracle that very night.

Miracle # 1: As I finished my message and the students began to pray, a young lady came and stood in front of me. I had noticed in our short time of being there that this girl was very shy. She wore thick glasses and when she took her glasses off, her eyes crossed severely. The doctors told her they could do nothing for her. Her name was Priya. As Priya stood in front of me, she began to cry, took her glasses off and pointed at her eyes. I very simply placed my thumbs on each of Priya's eyes and prayed, "Lord Jesus, if you are going to give me twelve miracles, I want this to be number one." Although I felt the Lord touch Priya at that moment, I didn't see an immediate miracle. Priya went over and sat on the floor against the wall and began to cry. The following morning Loretta and I were seated at the breakfast table with the Pastor's wife when we heard the front door open. Priya came walking in and stood next to my chair. I looked up into her smiling face. I didn't realize exactly what had happened until the Pastor's wife began to cry. Priya began to explain that when she looked in the mirror that morning she realized that she did not have her glasses on and that her eyes were no longer crossing, but perfectly straight. I jumped out of my chair and Priya and I shouted and rejoiced together about what God had done.

Miracle #2: There was a young man with his middle finger crooked and out of joint. He was prayed for in the service by Micah and Zachary Hicks, two brothers from my home church who had traveled with us. Upon being prayed for, the young man's finger POPPED and went straight! He could immediately make a fist which he could not do before. The rest of the time that we were there he would pose for pictures with all ten fingers stretched out for us to see.

Miracle #3: One of our students was a young lady who had lived with severe pain in her stomach and down the right side of her body since she was a little girl. I prayed several times for her over the course of a week but nothing would change. Finally, I prayed again and said, "In the name of Jesus, I curse this pain to the root!" She testified five days later that she had been without pain for five straight days for the first time in her life! (and without pain until now)

Miracle #4: One young lady had been very sickly and weak. She was lying on the floor in the church one evening during the worship service. I saw her and was moved with compassion because of her weakened condition. She did not even know I had entered the church because she had her eyes closed and was weeping. I went to her and lay my hand on her stomach. When I did, her entire body jumped off the floor and she was filled with the Holy Ghost for the first time and began speaking in tongues right then! When she got up from the floor she began to feel her abdomen and press on it. Her eyes became wide and she said, "It is different! It is different!" She has been well since then! Miracle #5: This miracle was also pertaining to this same young woman. The next morning after her physical healing she came to me excited and amazed at a telephone call she had just received. She related to me some history of how her father had loaned money to some people before his death. After his death, however, the people who had borrowed the money denied that they had ever taken anything, leaving her mother and their family in a strained financial situation. On this particular morning when the telephone rang at the Bible school, it was Deepika's mother. She told her daughter that the people who denied ever taking any money had suddenly come to their home returning the money they had borrowed in the first place. God was breaking chains in ways that we never even prayed for!

These are only five of the amazing miracle that we saw take place. The faith of those students grabbed hold of that simple word I have them. We began to receive phone calls from people that we did not even know asking us to pray over the phone because they had heard about twelve miracles that would take place. We even went over to some people's house that we did not know to pray for a small boy who had terribly high fever and was very sick. He had been taken to the hospital but no one knew what the problem was. We prayed in faith for his little body, and the fever broke. He began improving from then on.

    Oh my dear friends, God is so amazing. I have been overwhelmed watching God do HIS work. It is incredible what can take place when simple faith arises. Have faith in God, for 'nothing is impossible with HIM!"

THE REAL PEOPLE OF GOD!

SEPTEMBER, 2010

This was my eleventh trip to India in five years. The power of God was strong in the first service we held. I had just told the students about "twelve miracles" and miracles were already happening. I was preaching when I suddenly began to prophesy. Before I finished, the students in the Bible School began to jump and shout. God was moving in our midst! I looked up and saw a Sikh man standing in the doorway at the back of the Sanctuary. He was watching what was happening in our service. I can only imagine what he must have been thinking as the students prayed, jumped and shouted all over the room. I alerted Pastor Prakash to the Sikh man's presence, and he quickly went to speak to the man. Later, when the service was over, Pastor Prakash related to us the man's story. The Sikh man said, "Sir, I have been praying to know the real God and the real people of God. As I drove in front of your church tonight, the tire on my car suddenly went flat. When I got out of my car to check the tire, I heard so much noise coming from here that I had to check it out. I came over and have been watching what is happening here. Sir, these are the real people of God! I wish that my people worshipped like this! I wish we had a church like this in my village!" One of these days, God is going to let me see what happened to that man who saw the "real people of God."

WHEN IS IT MY TURN?!

YEAR: 2010

The Presence of the Lord flooded the second session of our Bible school class. Normally the session lasts for forty-five minutes, but on this day we were lost in the Presence of the Lord for two hours. Several were filled with the Holy Ghost and experiencing the true and living God in a way they never had before. After the extended "class" ended, Mama Loretta and I sat down on a small sofa in the sanctuary and began talking about what God had done. We were rejoicing over those who had been filled with the Spirit when we heard someone wailing. The youngest of our students was a girl seventeen years of age. She entered the church nearly dragging a girl with her who could interpret to us what she wanted to say. Through her wailing and tears she expressed to us that she wanted desperately to be filled with the Holy Ghost. I will never forget the agony in her voice as she cried out, "When is it my turn to be filled with the Holy Ghost?!" I replied to her, "Anytime is the right time for God to fill you! Right now is a perfect time."

    Her wailing and crying had attracted the attention of some of the other young ladies who wanted to find out what was happening inside the church. Even though we had just come out of a two hour prayer meeting, I told the girls who had come back into the church to join hands in a circle. We simply began to praise God for who He is and within moments the young lady who was so desperate for God was speaking in the most glorious heavenly language! For the next one and a half hours, Mama Loretta and I prayed with these hungry souls. Others began to filter in as they heard the sounds of prayer coming from the sanctuary. Nine of the ladies were filled with the Holy Ghost that afternoon. How sweet it is when only one person develops a true hunger for God.

Pilgrim, You'll Go Far

Seema, one of the ladies from Nepal, told Pastor Prakash that during this time of prayer she looked up and saw me in a white dress. She said there was so much light around me that even my hair looked white. In reality, I was wearing a black dress that day, but the Lord was letting Seema see something in the Spirit that would bless both of us. At the time, I did not know what she had seen. All I knew was that she came over to me and fell at my feet, clutching them and sobbing. I was so moved by her love that we wept together. This precious young woman was at one time filled with evil spirits and called insane by her family and friends, but hallelujah, not anymore! The love of Jesus shines brightly in her countenance and on this wonderful day she was filled with the Spirit of God. How beautiful it is to watch one's life changed from darkness to light.

The following day Mama Loretta hugged all the students and said goodbye as she left for America. I was staying, along with two young men from my church, for six weeks longer than Mama could stay. A couple of days after she had been gone we held our usual Sunday morning church service. The worship time was glorious. The Presence of the Lord was in our midst. I was worshipping the Lord with eyes closed and hands raised when suddenly I heard Mama Loretta's voice say very clearly and loudly in the manner she does, "JESUS!" It was so real that I opened my eyes to turn and look at her forgetting that she was not there. I then smiled realizing that she was still very much with us in the Spirit. I did not tell anyone what I had heard but it was confirmed as soon as church was over. Seema came with three other girls wanting to tell me something they had all heard during the service. They related to me the exact same experience that I had during the worship time. They said, "We heard 'Loretta Ma'am' and she said JESUS!" We were ecstatic as we all confirmed to each other that we had heard the same thing. There is no time or distance in the Spirit and we learned that and experienced it that day. Mama Loretta was now in America, but still with us in the Spirit in India. It was glorious to watch those young ladies learn that they had heard in the Spirit. It was thrilling to watch their faces light up as they realized they were growing in God and experiencing the Supernatural ways in which He works. It was now "THEIR TURN!"

SISTER PROMELA

YEAR: 2010

"*Precious memories, how they linger, how they ever flood my soul. In the stillness of the midnight, precious, sacred scenes unfold.*" If we ever had a precious friend in the nation of India it was Sister Promela. I look back at moments with Sister Promela and I have to either weep or smile. Those precious moments become even sweeter as the years stretch on. Recounting her story is precious beyond compare.

Sister Promela was a minister of the Gospel, even though her husband was not a Godly man, she pursued God. She pursued Him for herself. She pursued Him for her children. Sister Promela was an evangelist. She especially loved to work with children. She never stood on large stages, or preached to overwhelming crowds, but she loved Jesus. Her life was not one of ease, but you could see

Jesus in her smile. When she smiled, her entire face lit up.

    Our dear Sister Promela became sick and was diagnosed with cancer. Her battle with cancer was hard. She seemed to get better for a while, and then she heard the words that no one wants to hear, "The cancer is back." We had been in India for about a month in 2010 and had already been called to Sister Promela's house several times to pray. She was laying on her bed unable to fully communicate with anyone. She was moaning in pain and could not sit up, stand or walk. She had been unable to walk for nearly a year because of the cancer. We prayed and she would improve. The reason she would not let go was because of her family. There were some things that needed to be set right, and she would not go on into Eternity until they were. Her family began to tell us accounts of evil spirits that had been tormenting their home. They told of seeing a demonic old woman sitting on top of a brick wall outside their house. They told of it sounding like someone running straight through their house screaming. Their mother was dying and they were afraid. We knew we could not allow the devil to destroy this home with fear, so a group of us went over to Sister Promela's house and took communion. We then began to walk through the house praying, singing and declaring victory in the name of Jesus. I stood out in the yard and shook my finger in Sister Promela's son's face and those of his friends and told them they had better stop playing games with God. I told that I was going to pray that every time they got into drugs and sin that they would see my finger shaking in their faces. They kind of laughed at me, but that was only because they did not know how else to react. From that day, the tormenting spirits left the home.

At the end of October, we received a call that Sister Promela's kidneys had shut down. She had been taken to the hospital for her last moments here on Earth. The Doctor said she was in Stage 4 of her cancer and would pass very soon. When your kidneys shut down, you generally have about twenty-four hours left to live. We went to the hospital on Saturday niht, twenty-four hours after her kidneys had shut down. To be honest, I did not want to go to the hospital. I had never been with someone when they passed away. Nothing in me wanted to be there, but Mama Loretta told me I needed to go. When we walked into Sister Promela's hospital room we knew she was dying. Mama Loretta stood at the end of her bed and touched her feet. I stood at the head of her bed with arms around her daughter, Isha. Isha and I are close to the same age. It was difficult to stand there with her imagining the circumstances being flipped and it being my mother in that bed. I began to softly sing, *"What a friend we have in Jesus, all our sins and griefs to bear. What a privilege to carry everything to God in prayer."* Sister Promela had been looking at things in the room that were not visible to us. She had been kind of talking to angels that we could not see. We knew she was about to be with Jesus, but suddenly as we began to pray and sing, the presence of the Lord filled the room. Miraculously, Sister Promela came to her senses. She motioned to her daughter that she wanted help to get to the bathroom. We did not really know what was happening but we excused ourselves from the room to give her privacy and told her that we would see her later, fully expecting the "later" to be when we got to Heaven.

A miracle had taken place for the sake of Sister Promela's family. When we received a phone call the next morning that her kidneys were functioning again, we were amazed to say the least. Everyone was completely amazed, including the doctors. Sister Promela told us that she was going in to the grave that night, but the Lord pulled her out. She went from kidneys being shut down to kidneys functioning. She went from needing oxygen to pulling the oxygen out of her nose. She went from not being able to walk to walking down the hall to the x-ray department. They sent her home from the hospital a couple of days later. We went over to Sister Promela's house a few days later for a 'Thanksgiving service.' We all crowded into that little two room house. The walls were bare bricks and the bed took up most of the room. We pulled plastic chairs in around the bed and others sat on the bed with Sister Promela. Having come from death's door, we both cried and laughed as she lay there on her bed with arms raised high to Heaven thanking Jesus for His goodness.

There were things that Sister Promela wanted to do in her family before she left this Earth. She had made the statement that she was not happy with some things and wanted the chance to work on them. The grace of God will never be understood. Oh the depths at which God loves His children! That he would love so much to allow a dear, sweet mother to come back from the brink of death to take care of some things in her family. Things were much more peaceful when Sister Promela went home to be with Jesus a little over a month later. PRECIOUS MEMORIES, HOW THEY LINGER!

SEEMA AND THE SHOES

YEAR: 2010

There was a beautiful student at the Bible School from Nepal named Seema. She and I were the same age. From the moment I arrived, this precious student loved me. Seema poured her love out without knowing anything about me. She would hug me every possible chance she got. She would move from wherever she was just to be close to where I was sitting. She would even look at me adoringly, like a child looking at a mother. One day during an outpouring of God's Spirit, the Lord showed something to Seema. She told me later, through an interpreter, that when I walked in the room I was wearing a long white dress. She said there was so much light coming from me that she could just barely see my face. (I was actually wearing an all-black dress that day) At that moment Seema came over and threw herself at my feet. She clutched them and then drenched them with her tears. I have been completely covered since coming here by Seema's love.

It was the final Sunday that I would be in India on this trip. Even though I had resolved not to cry, I failed at my resolution when Seema came to my room. I had called her to my room because I wanted to give her something. I have been re-organizing and re-packing my stuff getting ready to leave. I had brought a pair of nice, black, dress shoes with me but because of gifts given to me on my Birthday the space in my suitcases was limited. I decided to see if my shoes would fit Seema since she was small in stature. (What can I say? I have small feet.) When she came to my room I held the shoes out to her. She immediately backed up against the wall saying, "No, no, no, and no." Her eyes were flooded with tears. I had to call an interpreter to find out why she reacted that way. I told her through the interpreter that I wanted her to see if these shoes would fit her because I didn't have room to take them home. She looked up at me, with tears streaming down her face and said, "But, I don't have anything to give YOU." This is the moment I failed at my resolution NOT to cry. I grabbed my precious friend, hugged her closely and said, "You smothered me with your love before you even knew me, and that was more than I deserved. You have loved me every moment I have been here and I couldn't ask for anything more precious than that!" Seema and I then cried together.

We have ONE who loved us before we knew HIM......and it was and is undeserved love. Let's be faithful to take our shoes, put them on our feet and walk out this life loving HIM in return. Isaiah 52:7 says, "HOW BEAUTIFUL upon the mountains are the feet of him that bringeth good tidings, that publisheth peace;…that publisheth salvation; that saith unto Zion, Thy God reigneth!"

YOU CAN'T COME IN

YEAR: 2010

Delays are practically inevitable when you travel internationally. In the nations of India and Nepal, however, those delays seem more prevalent than elsewhere. I have had to learn over the years not to expect things to happen as quickly as they do in America and it has been a point of frustration for us many times. We were once again in Poligenj, which is one of our favorite places near the border of Nepal where we stay at Pastor Prakash's family farm. Our plans were to leave the house at 5:30 a.m. to head toward Nepal for a meeting we were to preach that afternoon. When the early hour came, Mama Loretta and I were ready to go, but of course, everyone else was moving according to what we lovingly refer to as "Indian time." I kept having a feeling that we would not be going into Nepal that day. We finally left the house around 7:00 and drove to the border. The gates were closed. It took us an hour driving around from place to place to find the right official to let us in the first gate. We went through that initial barricade, but upon reaching the official immigration point, we were told that there had been changes made concerning Tourist visas. We could no longer come in and out of the country in the same day. The immigration officer told us that if we crossed the border, we would have to stay the night in the country and then we could come back across. We discussed it, but did not feel that we needed to stay the night.

After a long morning we turned around and drove back to the family farm at Poligenj. The truth is, we were rather disappointed because there had been nearly two-hundred people waiting for us to come preach the Gospel. Later that evening the three Nepali pastors, with whom we would have held the meeting that day, showed up at the Pastor's house in Poligenj. The pastors told us that they went ahead with the meetings that day and God had touched the people. They also told us that the following day there would be no travel allowed into or out of Nepal and that no vehicles would be moving due to some government rally. We realized then how God had been leading us not to go in and stay the night in the country. If we had, we would not have been allowed out for another day which would have messed up our travel itinerary. I have truly been amazed over the years at the ways in which God has kept us where He wants us.

A BREATH OF AIR

YEAR: 2012

The Lord has continually amazed me at the doors He has opened for me in ministry. Without telling anyone that I was "a preacher," I have stayed busy traveling and preaching more than I would have ever imagined. One such door of ministry opened to me in the small town of Lucedale in south Mississippi. Mama Loretta and I traveled there for a Missions Conference we had been invited to. The Conference was great and we were being blessed and encouraged. As we stood in line for lunch on one of the days, there was a young lady in line behind us. She made some comment about liking my hair and a conversation ensued. In the course of the next few days, we had invited the young lady, whose name is DeAdra, to travel to India with us after she graduated from high school. With that invitation, and DeAdra's acceptance of it, we managed to give her mother the proverbial heart attack.

In March of 2012, DeAdra was out of school and ready to go. When she was a child, she had major issues with asthma and had to consistently use an inhaler. Over time, her need for an inhaler had been almost nonexistent. DeAdra's mother, Connie, was insistent that her daughter take an inhaler to India because of the description I had given them of the poor air quality. Little did we know the scare and the miracle that awaited us surrounding that little inhaler.

We arrived safely in India and all was going according as planned. The Northern part of India where we work is known as the "Bread Basket" because of the farming industry, especially that of wheat. At that particular time of the year, they are in full swing of the wheat harvest. We all packed a couple of changes of clothing into an overnight bag, piled into the car and took off for a five hour drive to a village church. DeAdra, not having needed her inhaler for so long, never thought to put it in into her overnight bag. After arriving at the village, having dinner with the wonderful people and seeing God touch lives in the church service that evening, we were finally able to lie down for some rest. We were exhausted since we had only just arrived in India a couple of days before and jet lag was overwhelming our bodies. The conditions of our room were not fancy. We did have a bed which lifted us off of the floor, but it was simply made of a piece of plywood with a sheet laid over it. There was no mattress. The only thing soft was the neck pillow we had brought with us in traveling but we did not complain. We were tired and so the three of us lay down on our plywood bed. It was not too bad. At least we had a fan over us to keep the air moving which lessened the mosquito attacks. All three of us dozed off almost immediately, but then the electricity went off, and you were suddenly made aware of the poorness of the air quality in the room. We were literally in a house in the middle of wheat fields. We had walked down a narrow, dirt path alongside wheat fields that evening to get to the house we were to stay in. When the fan stopped, the air began to get kind of thick from the harvesting and the burning of harvested fields around us. DeAdra sat up suddenly in the bed. In my half asleep condition I asked her if she was okay. She replied that she felt like her asthma was acting up a little. To be honest, we said a quick prayer and then dozed again as jet lag took over. DeAdra, however, did not lay back down. Fortunately, the electricity came back on fairly quickly. We realized that DeAdra was getting up. She pulled a chair into the middle of the room and sat underneath the fan. We could tell she was having difficulty breathing by the way she would try to get a full breath of air. She was being brave, saying that she thought it was getting better, but we knew things were getting kind of serious.

    It was a little after midnight when Mama Loretta went to find Pastor Prakash. At this point, DeAdra was starting to make a wheezing sound. We talked with the Pastor who told us that the closest hospital was over an hour away. We were in a rather remote area and he did not feel that any little pharmacy in the village town would have what DeAdra needed. I was honestly becoming very concerned. I knew that we were in need desperately of a miracle. We climbed into the car with our young, wheezing friend and took off, not knowing exactly where we were going or what we would find. Mama Loretta and I were sitting on either side of DeAdra in the back seat. We were praying under our breath and praying aloud. Our words were mixing with the sounds of DeAdra trying to get a breath of air. I knew if anything happened to this dear girl, I would never be able to forgive myself.

Pastor Prakash's eldest son, Blesson, was driving the car. He kept stopping by the common, small pharmacy stands that you can find in India asking for something that would help DeAdra. To our dismay, each time he asked about an inhaler, the shop keeper would shake their heads no. Blesson would get back in the car and try again. DeAdra's breathing, or lack of it, had gotten to the point that we were all getting quite worried. I was ready for Blesson to take off driving at one hundred miles an hour to reach the hospital an hour away. Blesson, pulled the car around the next street corner and stopped again! I was starting to get frustrated with the seeming waste of time, but as he stopped the car this time, I saw a royal blue sign on the top of a house. It was a sign in the middle of "remote-ville" India. It was a wonderful sign that read, "Asthma Specialist of North India." We were in shock that such a place would exist in what seemed to be an impossible location. Blesson began ringing the bell on the outside of the gate. He had to ring it several times because it was very late and people were sleeping. Suddenly, the home owner appeared. Blesson related to him our situation. To our utter amazement, the home owner/shop keeper pulled some keys out of his pocket, unlocked the little shop on the side of his house and handed an inhaler to Blesson. Blesson ran to the car and handed it to DeAdra, not even knowing if this was the thing she needed. DeAdra, recognizing it, knew what to do and very quickly used the miraculous inhaler. Immediately she was able to breathe a nice big breath of air. Immediately all of our fear dissolved into the peace of knowing that God had just provided us with a miracle. Perhaps it was not the kind of miracle we had expected, but it was the kind of miracle that made an impact for a lifetime. We were able to turn the car around and go right back to our plywood board bed and get a little rest.

Those of us involved in this situation have talked with each other about the events that took place that night. We all still ask questions, "Could it have been? Was it really…?" We have all come to the same conclusion that it was truly a miracle from God and are convinced that if we returned to that same spot in India today that we would not find a royal blue sign lit up on the top of a house stating that there was an Asthma specialist available. Miracles come in all shapes and sizes and this one still leaves us shaking our head at the incredible way God provided a breath of air.

SISTER BUBBLY

YEAR: 2012

It was April 12, 2012. We were holding a meeting in Ambala City, Haryana, located in North India. Suddenly, at the back of the church, we saw Pastor Tara, one of the pastors we work with, come in. He was basically carrying his wife, Bubbly, into the building. Sister Bubbly had to lay on the floor at the back of the church because she was in so much pain and was so weak. It was apparent that life was leaving her body. Mama Loretta and I, and a young sister with us named DeAdra, went to the back of the church and prayed for our dear Sister Bubbly.

One year later we returned to Ambala City. Meetings had been scheduled for us. We traveled an hour and a half to hold a meeting in a village church. When we arrived we followed Pastor Tara into an alley. We walked alongside water buffalo to reach his house. Upon reaching his front door, we were met by a smiling Sister Bubbly. They brought refreshments to us in typical Indian fashion and custom and then said they wanted to share their testimony with us. We were not aware of all that had happened in the previous year.

    Prior to bringing Sister Bubbly in and laying her on the church floor, Pastor Tara had taken her from hospital to hospital. She had contracted serious Typhoid fever and had gone into double kidney failure. She had been taken to the largest and most famous hospital in the North India area called PGI. The doctors told Sister Bubbly that she would have to have both kidneys transplanted. They needed a certain amount of money or a certain government card to be able to stay in the hospital. Otherwise, they were told to return home and let her say her goodbyes to family and friends. Pastor Tara and Sister Bubbly and their two small children had been through so much for their faith in Christ. They had even been surrounded in their own home by the Hindus in their village and threatened. The Hindus threatened to burn them in their home if they did not stop preaching. It was only by a miracle of God that their lives were spared. So, upon Sister Bubbly receiving this diagnosis of death, the villagers all began to watch and see what would happen to this Christian.

Pastor Tara had done all he could do for his wife. They had no money, no hope in this world. Their only hope was Jesus. They heard that we had come to Ambala City, so they left everything and said, "Lord Jesus, You are our only hope!" This is the point at which we came into their story. When Pastor Tara came in to church carrying his wife, we did not know what they had been through. We did not know the doctor's diagnosis. We did not know the testing of their faith that they had been through. We did however know that Jesus is our Healer.

They shared with us as we sat in their home one year after praying and believing with them. From that very night that we prayed, Sister Bubbly was able to eat food, which she had not been able to do. They were not able to stay for the rest of the meetings because she was so weak, so they returned home. Sister Bubbly had been at death's door, but she began to improve. The same doctor who told her to go home and say goodbye called them back to the hospital saying that he would like to run more tests on Sister Bubbly. They went to the hospital. This Hindu doctor ran the tests. He then sat with them in an office waiting on the results. When the doctor received the new tests results and looked at them. He was not able to remain in his seat. He stood up, shocked, and said, "I have never seen anything like this in my life! FROM WHERE DID YOU GET THESE BRAND NEW KIDNEYS?!" Pastor Tara began to ask the doctor questions about what they needed to do. The doctor told them she had a perfectly clear bill of health, two brand new kidneys, needed no medicine, could eat anything she wanted and to go home and enjoy her life and family.

    Pastor Tara and Sister Bubbly, in earthly terms, have nothing. However, in a heavenly sense of things, they have it all. They have life, health and Godliness. Incidentally, Pastor Tara and Sister Bubbly have many new Believers in their church because they saw the miracle that God performed in the life of this "Christian." We went to their church after they shared this incredible, miraculous testimony and saw a courtyard filled with people who have come to God because of their trial of fire. God's ways are certainly higher than ours. Pastor Tara and Sister Bubbly came through that fire and have come out as pure gold.

THE LAND OF MANY BATTLES

YEAR: 2013

It seems there is always a spiritual battle to fight in the nation of India. Being a land of millions of idol gods, you can imagine the spiritual darkness that prevails, and yet, the true people of God shine brightly. The lines are not blurred at all between right and wrong. You either belong wholeheartedly to the One True God or you do not. I have learned over the years that the enemy is not as smart as people give him credit for. He gives himself away. Anytime we are in a meeting, I will watch the crowd as we begin to praise and worship God. I scan the people for any sign of the enemy. You know the old adage, "the eyes are the window to the soul." It is a true saying. Whenever there is mixture in someone's life, they are not able to keep their eyes closed when attempting to pray. They will try to pray, but their eyes will begin to roll back in their head until you see only the whites of their eyes. You can actually watch as the battle is waged. The person will sort of shake themselves, open their eyes, look around and then try to close them in prayer again.

In this one particular gathering of people, I had noticed a very slender man. The previous night I had watched him closely as his eyes rolled back in his head. I noticed his mouth was moving but he was not actually praying any words. I knew this was a bigger stronghold than normal. On this day we were praying for people who wanted to be filled with the Holy Ghost. Four had already been filled. God was moving in our midst. I had also been watching three young ladies during that week, not because they couldn't keep their eyes closed, but because they were the saddest looking three I had ever seen. There was never a smile, never a glimmer in their eye, and they kept their chins down barely looking up at anyone. I knew there had to be something in their life that was keeping them so bound. I began to pray with these three young ladies. As we were praying, the slender man, whom I had been watching, worked his way up to the front and began to pray for people as well. I saw him and immediately felt like making him sit down. Then, to my shock, I saw as this man laid his hand on one of the girls I had also been watching. The girl went crazy. She began to pull at his hand trying to get it off of her head. She was screaming and being controlled by this man. The man hit the girl on top of the head and then pulled his hand back and held it about ten inches from the top of her head. I watched as he waved his hand like a snake-charmer over the top of the girls head and, although the girl's eyes were closed, her head followed his hand around. It had all happened so fast but I had seen enough! The Prophetess Deborah was standing tall on the inside on the inside of me. I stepped over to that situation, grabbed the girl and swung her around and broke that hold he had. I looked at Pastor Prakash and said forcefully, "Who is that man?! Get him out of here!" The girl was shaking and didn't know what had happened. I told her in Hindi to begin to speak the name of Jesus. Pastor Prakash actually did not know the slender man, only that he claimed to be a pastor. He wasn't a true pastor. He was full of the devil and had been using witchcraft powers over the three young ladies I had been watching so closely. I whirled around to the man and began to shake my finger in his face as I prayed in the Spirit. He backed up against the pulpit, folded his hands and tried to act religious. I turned my attention back on the three girls and prayed with them and comforted them. I realized that the entire crowd, who had been praying to be filled with the Spirit, was now not praying and simply watching the scene. If ever I have experienced a "taking back" of what the enemy was stealing, it was that moment. I realized at that moment, from previous experiences in India, that if this situation was not addressed people would be questioning the moving of the Holy Ghost. They would be left with questions about the Spirit all together. So, I stepped into the middle of the circle people had formed and boldly proclaimed, "The enemy is trying to steal from us today but I am not going to let him!" I asked how many had been filled with the Spirit as we were praying and hands went up everywhere. "See," I said, "God has filled you with His Spirit, and the enemy came in to try to steal, kill and destroy us today, but Jesus came to give us LIFE and He has done so. We are going to turn our attention away from what the enemy did and back toward Jesus and we are going to praise Him for His Spirit!" My, my, my, those people turned their eyes back on Jesus and we took back our newly gained victory. I saw smiles on those three girls' faces after that morning. They were big, beautiful smiles.

CONCLUSION:

THE REALITY OF MISSIONS

Whenever Mama Loretta and I travel together, we usually end up talking, crying and praying before we go to sleep at night. On one particular trip we had done this for several nights in a row. It was 2:00 a.m. and we were talking about the things of God and crying when out of the corner of my eye I see a shadow crawling up the walk in the dark. We turned the light on to find a ten inch, rather plump lizard climbing up the wall. I am sure it would have been quite comical to watch us jumping around and climbing all over the bed trying to catch the silly thing! In the end, all worked out and we let the critter go out the window, even though we were on the second story of the building. After that, the only critters we had to fight were the mosquitoes. They are so pesky! I counted all the mosquito bites on this night and found a total of fifty-two. Unfortunately, I always acquire more.

It is so hot many times in India and the electricity does not stay on. Even with a fan the air is hot. On my first trip to India, I would wake up every night having soaked my pajamas, pillow and sheet with sweat. It was so hot that I would get up at 2:00 a.m. to take a cold shower.

    India is also a country that is not very clean. There aren't public trash bins for throwing your garbage away. Everyone simply throws their trash on the ground or lets it blow out the window of the vehicle they are in. Because of so many people in a small land mass, the air space across India is very polluted. You can take a bucket bath and then go outside to the market. In just a short time, your fingernails will look like you have been digging in the dirt and forgot to clean them. Another reality of the air pollution is that after being out in the market place you can blow your nose and what comes out is black. I can only imagine what the people of India must breathe into their lungs throughout their lives.

    These are just a few of the realities of the mission field. I did not go to India to make all the water clean or to sweep the streets free of litter or to ban all lizards from the houses. I did, however, go to India because the God who created me and fashioned me in His likeness called me to take His Gospel, His message, to the uttermost parts of this Earth. The reality of God's plan staggers me at times. That God would choose a young girl like me, who is tearful at times, afraid at times, giggling at times, is amazing and beyond my comprehension. I find reality and understanding as I begin to read Jeremiah and hear God calling his name and saying, "I have called you to the nations." One might quickly conclude, 'if God called me, then He must be going to give me a private jet and a palace when I get to where He is sending me.' We have the reality of Isaiah's call, Esther's assignment, Ezekiel's visions and Daniel's lions' den to nullify those kinds of sentiments. We might still laugh and chase the lizards and giggle when riding the bicycle rickshaw, but the reality is He has called us. He is still saying, "Who will go, FOR ME?" I decided I would. I want to be able to say like Jesus said, "I have come to do Thy will, O God!"

After ten years of laboring in the Nations, I find that the task is greater than I imagined. I have laughed many times, but I have cried more. I can now say that I have heard the cries of the Nations. When I went to India, I did not know that millions of children live on the garbage heaps and are called the trash pickers or untouchables. I did not know that people were worshipping monkeys and cows and snakes and rats and everything else you can imagine. I did not know that millions sleep on the streets every night and many die there. I did not know that little girls are either killed or sold as prostitutes before they are ten years old. I did not know the untold atrocities that go on in the Nations. I DID NOT KNOW! All I know is, the God of all flesh, who is the Treasure in this earthen vessel of mine, sent me to them. This God came to seek and to save the lost one, of whom there are so many. I have prayed with and for people on trains, in taxis, on airplanes, on the streets, in rickshaws and in places of business. My assignment is to get these people to the living God. There was a time when I could safely say, "I do not know." Now, however, I DO KNOW, and I carry the weight of reaching them with the greatest message of all, that God so loved the world. Until He changes my assignment, I will labor faithfully in His harvest field in the Nations of this world. Until the day when I can say, like my Lord said, "It is finished."

Made in the USA
Charleston, SC
30 July 2015